At Issue

Nuclear Anxiety

Other Books in the At Issue Series

Athlete Activism
Food Security
Genocide
Mob Rule or the Wisdom of the Crowd?
Money Laundering
Open Borders
Pandemics and Outbreaks
Sexual Consent
Student Debt
Universal Health Care
Vaccination

Nuclear Anxiety

Haq Kamar, Book Editor

Published in 2021 by Greenhaven Publishing, LLC
353 3rd Avenue, Suite 255, New York, NY 10010

First Edition

Articles in Greenhaven Publishing anthologies are often edited for length to meet page requirements. In addition, original titles of these works are changed to clearly present the main thesis and to explicitly indicate the author's opinion. Every effort is made to ensure that Greenhaven Publishing accurately reflects the original intent of the authors. Every effort has been made to trace the owners of the copyrighted material.

Cover image: Romolo Tavani/Shutterstock.com

Library of Congress Cataloging-in-Publication Data

Names: Kamar, Haq, editor.
Title: Nuclear anxiety / Haq Kamar.
Description: First Edition. | New York : Greenhaven Publishing, 2020. | Series: At issue | Includes bibliographical references and index. | Audience: Grades 9–12.
Identifiers: LCCN 2020004050 | ISBN 9781534507425 (library binding) | ISBN 9781534507418 (paperback)
Subjects: LCSH: Anxiety—Social aspects. | Nuclear warfare—Psychological aspects. | Nuclear warfare—History. | World politics.
Classification: LCC HM1033 .N83 2020 | DDC 152.4/6—dc23
LC record available at https://lccn.loc.gov/2020004050

Manufactured in the United States of America

Website: http://greenhavenpublishing.com

Contents

Introduction

In the full span of human history, nuclear weapons are a very recent development. In 1938, German scientists Otto Hahn, Lise Meitner, and Fritz Strassman initially discovered the technology of nuclear fission in Berlin, Germany.[1] Nuclear fission is when an atom of radioactive material splits into lighter atoms, releasing a huge amount of energy in the process. Some weapons developed later would go on to use a mixture of fission and fusion (which is the exact opposite process: fusing lighter radioactive atoms to create a large atom), but this initial discovery was the stepping-stone towards nuclear weaponization.

America played a major role in weaponizing nuclear technology with the Manhattan Project (1939–1946), a conference of scientists tasked to research and develop nuclear weaponry. This endeavor eventually culminated in the first and only deployment of nuclear weaponry in human history thus far: the 1945 bombings by American forces in Hiroshima and Nagasaki, Japan. The attack decimated the cities, killing 70,000 in the initial blast. A recent study by the Department of Energy claims the five-year death toll may have reached or exceeded 200,000 people.[2] In the years following the end of World War II, the United States attempted to prevent the spread of nuclear weapons by proposing the Baruch Plan to the United Nations, named for the US representative to the UN Energy Commission, Bernard Baruch. At the address, Baruch said, "We are here to make a choice between the quick and the dead. That is our business...If we fail, then we have damned every man to be the slave of fear."[3] Ultimately, the plan failed to get unanimous support, and Baruch's words proved prophetic. The USSR obtained blueprints for nuclear weapons and tested their first nuclear bomb in 1949. Thus began the Cold War (1947–1991), a war of arms and attrition between the two superpowers—America and the Soviet Union—that drove the fear of nuclear destruction deep into the public psyche.

The attacks on Hiroshima and Nagasaki offered a first glimpse at this new level of savagery, and the Cold War would exacerbate and accelerate these fears further. The US and the Soviet Union scrambled to stockpile and develop the technology. The threat of total nuclear annihilation was held back solely because of how quickly it would devolve: A nuclear strike would beget a nuclear retaliation, and the entire world could perish in the crossfire. Thus, it seemed neither nuclear power would cast the first stone under the precarious premise of mutually assured destruction.

Even though no nuclear missiles were ever detonated during this conflict, the implicit threat echoed through political and civilian life. As each nuclear superpower amassed their stockpiles, some countries aligned themselves with one or the other—hoping that would keep their populaces out of the crossfire. Other allied states such as China, the United Kingdom, and France chased their own nuclear ambitions to maintain autonomy and deter foreign intervention under the same guise of mutual destruction. Civilians were privy to the political agendas of their leaders that centered on the nuclear threat, but it seemed there was no escape from this anxiety taking hold in other spheres of life. Many felt the need to take safety into their own hands, constructing nuclear bunkers for themselves in hopes of surviving the nuclear holocaust. Public schools would have regular drills in case of nuclear attack—much like the more familiar fire drills of today—and thus even young children were aware of the fragile state of the world.

International efforts to suppress nuclear weapons were revisited in the 1960s. Negotiations occurred amid worldwide protests for nuclear disarmament. It seemed the Cold War would finally wind down when the Nuclear Non-Proliferation Treaty (NPT) was endorsed by the United Nations in 1968 and eventually enforced starting in March 1970. Nuclear signatories pledged to reduce and eventually completely disarm their nuclear weapons, and non-nuclear signatories pledged they would never bear nuclear arms. Some countries have defied this treaty, but at the very least the biggest nuclear players—the US and Russia—have pledged to uphold this treaty, and the fear of nuclear destruction cooled down as a result.

But it seemed the peace was not meant to hold. For many adults today, the prevailing fear of catastrophic weapons of war in the current political climate began with the September 11 terror attacks that took place in the US in 2001. In their wake, the media and President George W. Bush claimed that the terrorist group al-Qaeda would soon follow with bigger weapons and bigger plans that would leave American democracy vulnerable.[4] Thus, "weapons of mass destruction" formed the *casus belli* of a war touted to be both a "pre-emptive strike" and a retaliation for the September 11 attacks. The enduring anxiety surrounding the possibility of malignant powers possessing and using weapons of mass destruction shaped yet another historical era for the US and beyond.

More recently, the election of American president Donald Trump in 2016 is considered by some to be the latest catalyst for nuclear anxiety. Indeed, Trump has long expressed a fascination regarding the use of nuclear weapons, dating back to the 1980s.[5] Yet all over the world, it seems nuclear stability is being called into question. North Korea in its secrecy is reportedly pushing a nuclear arms program and is the primary antagonist in President Trump's vision of a possible nuclear skirmish. Israel also maintains a nuclear stockpile in defiance of the Nonproliferation Treaty. Neither India nor Pakistan signed the NPT, and both are embroiled in a drawn-out border conflict in the Kashmir region, embodying their own microcosm of mutually assured destruction. It should come as no surprise that nuclear anxiety has reemerged to the greatest heights since the Cold War as a result of these conflicts.

To tackle this issue, *At Issue: Nuclear Anxiety* investigates the ways these anxieties affect society on a public level. Such fears permeate international policy in various corners of the world—from the Middle East, to America, to Korea. Viewpoint authors look at how these anxieties affect citizens on a personal level—both in terms of mental health and the kinds of relationships or connections people may form in light of such fear. Additionally, this volume examines possible solutions some viewpoint authors suggest to demystify this fear and perhaps give the anxious reader some solace in these tense times.

Notes

1. "Atomic Bomb History," *History,* May 16, 2019, https://www.history.com/topics/world-war-ii/atomic-bomb-history.
2. "The Manhattan Project: An Interactive History," US Department of Energy, https://www.osti.gov/opennet/manhattan-project-history/Events/1945/hiroshima.htm/.
3. Joshua Williams, "The Quick and the Dead," Carnegie Endowment for International Peace, June 16, 2005, https://carnegieendowment.org/publications/index.cfm?fa=view&id=17078&prog=zgp&proj=znpp.
4. Susan Moeller, "Weapons of Mass Destruction and the Media: Anatomy of a Failure," YaleGlobal Online, April 14, 2004, https://yaleglobal.yale.edu/content/weapons-mass-destruction-and-media-anatomy-failure.
5. Ron Rosenbaum, "Trump's Nuclear Experience," *Slate*, March 1, 2016, http://www.slate.com/articles/news_and_politics/the_spectator/2016/03/trump_s_nuclear_experience_advice_for_reagan_in_1987.html.

1

Hiroshima and the Lasting Impacts of Nuclear War

Becky Alexis-Martin

Becky Alexis-Martin is a lecturer of political and cultural geographies at Manchester Metropolitan University and a senior research fellow in human geography at the University of Southampton, both in the United Kingdom. Her research interests include the health and well-being of nuclear communities.

As the site of one of the only two nuclear attacks in human history, Hiroshima's residents lived, persevered, and grew from what others have only feared. Alexis-Martin's slice-of-life viewpoint—presented as a walk through the Hiroshima Peace Memorial Park—offers a broad glimpse into the various ways both residents and visitors connect with the legacy of the 1945 bombing. As with all things human, their relationships to this history are diverse and, at times, unexpected.

Hiroshima is flourishing. It has a population surpassing 1.19 million, a burgeoning gourmet scene, towering luxury shopping centres, and a trendy night life. It is a city of vibrant green boulevards and open spaces, entangled by the braided tributaries of the Ōta River. However it is also a city of memorialisation. Over 75 monuments, large and small, sprout like delicate mushrooms in parks and on sidewalks, scattered across the city as if by the wind. Whilst the city grows and evolves, the memory remains of

"Life After the Bomb: Exploring the Psychogeography of Hiroshima," by Becky Alexis-Martin, Guardian News and Media Limited, August 6, 2017. Reprinted by permission.

Hiroshima as the first place on Earth where nuclear weapons were used in warfare, on 6 August 1945.

The number of fatalities is not known, due to wartime population transience and the destruction of records in the blast. Estimates are in the region of 135,000 people, roughly equivalent to the population of Oxford. It is therefore unsurprising that many locals have Hibakusha veterans in their families. The Hibakusha community maintain a living collective memory of the bomb, sharing their atomic folktales similarly to the Kataribe storytellers, as a cautionary modern mythology against nuclear war.

It was assumed that nothing would grow within the bleak 1.6km blast-zone for 75 years. However, surrounding prefectures donated trees to Hiroshima. Fresh stems quickly pushed through the damaged earth, plants took root, and the branches of the Hibaku-jumoku, the survivor trees, unfurled leaves of weeping willow and oleander from budded stalks. The city has been rehabilitated, and it is challenging to imagine it as a place of devastation. Hiroshima Peace Memorial Park is a lush focal point of this re-greening process, and a unique human ecosystem has sprung up among the gingko trees and sussurating cicadas.

The park has its own distinctive psychogeography, providing a public space for complex emotions and experiences to be explored by locals and tourists. International visitors feature prominently around the larger memorials and cenotaph. They ring the delicate origami crane bell-pull within the Children's Peace Monument, take a few photographs of the cenotaph, stroll beside the Peace Pond, and then across the river to the A-bomb dome.

Distance is no indication of personal connection, and victims of Hiroshima have originated from across the USA, China and South East Asia. Thousands of Koreans died in Hiroshima: the men were forcibly conscripted and the women performed the duties of "comfort women." The monument and Cenotaph to Korean Victims are festooned with brightly coloured flowers and receive a constant trickle of visitors, many of whom are Korean. Swags of peace cranes garland the smaller memorials dotted about the park, and the fragrance of sandalwood and citron lingers, as incense is lit and local heads are respectfully bowed. Japanese schoolchildren come here to learn, and they sit in the shade of the trees at noon in civilised huddles, to eat lunch and chatter.

Many visit to reflect upon the atrocity of the bombing, but this attitude is not universal. I learned this during an encounter with an American man at the Ground Zero memorial, tucked away on a side-street beyond the boundaries of the park. We smiled at each other, as he shared his reasons for visiting, declared the power of the bomb to end the war, and the American soldiers, including his grandfather, whose lives were saved by this action. He was grateful for the bomb, but I was shocked at the way he had decided to make an emotional connection with this place.

However, the local community has a deep and profound connection to the park. Volunteers in distinctive uniforms meticulously maintain the place on a daily basis. This voluntary care of space escalates, as Hiroshima Peace Day draws near. Visit the park at 6am towards the end of July, and you will discover hordes of elderly people from the "Senior University," wearing sunhats and brandishing trowels. They crouch above the ground, plucking weeds from the soil with gloved fingers. Whilst they garden, trails of elegantly dressed office workers bisect the park at intervals, carrying files and parasols in delicately gloved hands. Commuting to work, this stretch of land has become another familiar part of the rhythm of their daily lives.

There are also spaces of conflict and deviance here. The Uyoku dantai are the Japanese extreme-far right. They call themselves the Society of Patriots and travel about in dark vans painted with worrying slogans. War crime denialists, they support historical revisionism, oppose socialism and want Japan to join the nuclear circus. Unfortunately, they cannot be arrested due to the protection of freedom of ideology by the Constitution of Japan. So they jeer from the sidelines of the park, and organise protests outside the A-Dome on Hiroshima Peace Day. To the consternation of many, they have been gaining popularity in recent years.

However, there is also a place of joy hidden within this park, on a dusty corner of dry earth behind the public toilets. Here, a group of elderly Japanese men meet every week-day morning, to crouch on battered wooden chairs and play board games. Some, but not all, are Hibakusha, but all of them look relaxed, and laugh loudly as they engage in drawn-out battles of Shogi and Go. They have created their own friendly-yet-private space within this park. As dusk sets in, they pack up their board games and fold up their little chairs and tables to go home. The cicadas grow louder, and a calmness settles over the park as twilight descends. Small clusters of local teenagers gather and relax in the evening's warmth. Faint sounds of conversation gradually dwindle to nothingness and the day draws to a close, reclaimed by the stillness of night. Our day in the park may be over, but the collective memory of the Hiroshima bombing forever remains.

2

America's Relationship to Nuclear Armament

Emanuel Pastreich

Emanuel Pastreich is an academic in South Korea. He currently serves as director of the Asia Institute and director of the Earth Management Institute in Cheonan.

Pastreich interviews Lawrence Wilkerson, who was the chief of staff to former Secretary of State Colin Powell. Wilkerson offers startling insights into the Trump administration, which is currently in charge of the biggest nuclear arsenal on the planet. Pastreich and Wilkerson go over the various factors that contribute to this new wave of American militarization, including US-China relations and the arms industry, as well as what America needs to do to de-escalate the international nuclear situation.

Emanuel Pastreich: What is the current status of the Intermediate-Range Nuclear Forces (INF) Treaty on nuclear weapons?

Lawrence Wilkerson: As you know, the United States pulled out of the INF medium-range nuclear weapons treaty with Russia in August and it plans a substantial buildup of these destabilizing weapons, above all in East Asia. This move is dangerous.

"America's Rush Back to Nuclear Weapons," by Emanuel Pastreich, Institute for Policy Studies, May 9, 2019. https://fpif.org/americas-rush-back-to-nuclear-weapons/.

The INF Treaty was far from perfect, but it had a broad appeal, including an appeal to many in the military, because it simply made sense.

That treaty between the United States and Russia encompassed all missiles, nuclear or conventional, ballistic or cruise, that had a range of between 500 and 5,500 kilometers. When the INF Treaty was signed in 1987, it helped to slow down a dangerous arms race. For the first time since the Cold War started, an entire class of nuclear weapons was eliminated.

Pastreich: Why do you think the United States withdrew?

Wilkerson: We no longer live in a rational world in which policy makers take a scientific approach to risk. Rather, policy making is dominated by irrational figures like John Bolton, the president's national security advisor, a man who hates arms control with a passion, who spends his days trying to find ways to undo the few restrictions that remain, and who would plunge the world into a completely new nuclear arms race.

This time, however, the competition won't be bilateral, just between the United States and the USSR. This time the race will be global, and we will see a nightmare world of instability, with a renewed risk of a nuclear holocaust as a result.

Pastreich: What's the background behind this drastic shift in American policy?

Wilkerson: Right now there are a huge number of intermediate range missiles stationed in Fujian Province, and elsewhere in southern China, which are aimed at Taiwan. We're talking about a missile for just about every square meter of every viable target in Taiwan. China was never a signatory to the INF Treaty because at the time its missile capacity was minimal and its nuclear weapons policy, which was set by Mao Zedong, was one of sufficiency to deter.

If there was a valid reason for the United States to withdraw from the current INF Treaty, it was this change in China's missile arsenal. China is most likely contemplating a new doctrine with regard to the use of nuclear weapons. That change has little to do with Russia and everything to do with the pressing need for a new nuclear weapons arms control regime.

Pastreich: You mean that China's actions were a reason for the United States to withdraw?

Wilkerson: In part, the changes in China were a factor. And Russia has been "cheating" with respect to the INF Treaty. Even more dangerous is Russia's publication of a military doctrine calling for blunting NATO's advantage in PGMs [precision guided munitions] by using short-range nuclear strikes. Russia has been building a missile inventory necessary to accomplish this doctrine.

There are of course other aspects of the problem. We find a mutual abuse of the INF Treaty, such as the United States putting ABM defenses and troops in former Warsaw Pact countries, thus moving the borders of NATO so that they are smack up against Russia's "near abroad." And now the United States refuses to talk about almost anything with Russia.

We see the proliferation of medium-range missiles among non-signatory countries (China, DPRK, Iran, Saudi Arabia, etc.) and also violations of the INF Treaty by both the original treaty signatories, who also happen to be the owners of the vast preponderance of nuclear weapons.

Pastreich: What do you think that should the United States have done then?

Wilkerson: Sadly, the United States kept complaining about what was imperfect about the treaty, but it made no effort to create something better, to fashion and gain support for an entirely new and more comprehensive nuclear arms control regime.

Instead, what the United States is accomplishing is the launch of a far more virulent arms race, one that could lead, some would argue inevitably, to the use of nuclear weapons in war.

It would have made better sense to maintain the treaty, or to declare it obsolete, in a bipartisan manner, and, in either case, to open negotiations to expand the treaty so as to include all nations that possess extensive stockpiles of intermediate range missiles—particularly those that also possessing nuclear weapon capability. From the point of view of smart arms control, of our children's future, and of the security of the United States and of the world, such an expanded and modernized, treaty would make perfect sense.

But Trump's national security advisor, John Bolton, doesn't do arms control. Moreover, Trump himself seems to disdain multilateral arrangements, sensible negotiations, and the type of astute diplomacy required to accomplish either. He seems to more-or-less follow Bolton and his desire for "a little nuclear war." While campaigning, Trump even suggested he believed the world would be better off if there were more, not fewer, nuclear weapons, and states that possessed them.

Pastreich: What can be done now to correct this mistake?

Wilkerson: I think you mean, given these clear realities what can be done to modify the behavior of an administration that has been opposed to arms control from the very start and that has done more and will do more to damage arms control efforts than any previous administration? How will we convince John Bolton and Mike Pompeo, who made their careers by opposing rational arms control treaties, that they don't need to abandon treaties but should rather expand them, multi-lateralize them, and seek new ones that do even more than the old ones did?

If we are talking about these individuals alone, the task is hopeless. They are beyond redemption. But democratic politics is not simply about individuals, whether it be presidents, national security advisors, or otherwise. There are cases in American history where extremist politicians have been brought into line by a shift in the mood and in the culture and by a weigh-in by the demos in accordance with such shifts.

What we need is to create again in Washington DC a nuclear arms control environment, a culture in which responsibility and strict regulation of nuclear weapons—and other weapons, as in the Conventional Forces in Europe Treaty—is accepted as a necessity. We need to ensure that such a development is a natural occurrence, that it is something that is not disdained, but rather anticipated.

At the end of the day, we need to negotiate a series of treaties that form a global overlapping system that includes all classes of nuclear weapons. We need to bring into this process pariah states like Israel and North Korea. Achieving that goal requires us to be tough at times. We must be ready to take a strong stand to insist that all nuclear weapon states must join the regime that will be established.

Pastreich: What is the thinking about nonproliferation and disarmament in the US military?

Wilkerson: The military makes the challenge even greater because there are large factions in the military who are hankering for a new nuclear arms race. Those generals and admirals want more money, and they want to build more missiles. Doing so will allow them to get their hands on some of the trillion-plus dollars allotted for new nuclear weapons by former President Obama.

Those officers want all sorts of nuclear and non-nuclear missiles, but the diversity in their demands does not mean that they are strategically imaginative. They are not.

All they want is more, more, and a little more. But we should also remember that there are some clear thinkers and some brave people devoted to the common good mixed in with them. They see the handwriting on the wall and they wish to avert nuclear war.

President Trump is highly susceptible to the military's siren call. The president has painted himself into multiple corners, and he seems to feel that he desperately needs the military to be president of the United States. Since he now faces opposition at almost every level of government and increasingly within the country, loyalty has become his first priority. He perceives the military to be overwhelmingly loyal to him and he wants to reward them.

This relationship between Trump and the military is dangerous because Trump is so ignorant about diplomacy and security, and at the same time he is increasingly desperate in his search for support. He does not care about global warming or nuclear war, but he is obsessed with his political standing. He desires above all to have people who will gather around him and listen to him speak. He is ultimately concerned with holding on to power.

Moreover, nuclear missiles, in particular, offer big juicy contracts that are not subject to much external review, and they empower the president—who is the one who can decide on his own whether or not to use them. So these weapons also feed Trump's ego.

But anyone with any understanding of nuclear weapons knows how close we have come to nuclear war in the past—even with treaties in place. Sadly, most educated citizens have no idea how different a world we will be living in once the nuclear weapon genie escapes from its bottle, especially as there is a whole new group of nations like Germany, Turkey, Iran, Japan, South Korea, Australia, Brazil, Indonesia, and so on, that have either in the past shown a desire for nuclear weapons or who could join in a future nuclear arms race.

Pastreich: The decision to withdraw from the INF treaty, and other agreements like the ABM Treaty, while simultaneously increasing the number of short-range nuclear missiles, seems as if it was made in meetings among Bolton, Pompeo and

Trump, with some input from the military. There were few, if any, congressional committees who debated the new policies, or summoned experts on nonproliferation for testimony.

Wilkerson: This unhealthy policy-making process seems to be intrinsic to the Trump administration. But the shift has been taking place for some time. The cause is not necessarily Trump.

H.L. Mencken wrote back in 1920 that one day, "...the White House will be adorned by a downright moron." Although that prediction was uncanny, it was not a matter of chance.

The current crescendo of incompetence is the product of a long-term structural and statutory shift that has encouraged a dysfunctional decision-making process.

We can see Trump's arbitrary use of power as the logical conclusion of the centralization of national security decision-making in the White House that dates back to the 1947 National Security Act. This concentration of power in the White House, and the decline of the power of the president's cabinet, as well as of the powerful congressional committees run by highly educated and focused political leaders like Jacob Javits or James Fulbright, have profoundly altered the process by which policy is formulated and decisions are made.

The next step came after Ronald Reagan both consolidated power in the executive and stripped other parts of the federal government of budgets and authority. He created a new policy landscape that was readily made use of by H. W. Bush, Bill Clinton, George W. Bush, and Barack Obama, with some slight variations. So, the original balance of powers among Congress, the judiciary, and the executive described in the constitution existed only by dint of institutional inertia. That balance was ready to be torn down—and was torn down like a rotten tree—by Trump's people.

Pastreich: How does this institutional shift relate to the seemingly endless wars the United States is involved in?

Wilkerson: Many members of Congress—and particularly powerful committee chairmen—are backed to the hilt by Lockheed Martin, Raytheon, Boeing, BAE, Grumman, General Dynamics, and other military contractors who are pursuing big-budget contracts with the government. This trend is true for both parties, but the Republicans practice it with greater abandonment. The coffers of these Congress members are essentially filled up by lobbyists who represent these merchants of war.

Pastreich: Although it seems irrelevant to lobbyists and influence peddlers, the constitution is supposed to be the manual that determines how the Federal government is run.

Wilkerson: The three branches of government are co-equal, but the legislative branch was clearly meant to be primus inter pares, and James Madison was quite adamant on that point.

The executive has become the overwhelmingly dominant branch. And now you have a specially selected Supreme Court and a court system that basically approves all of the executive branch's actions, domestic and foreign. The Congress, especially the Republican-dominated Senate, is incapable of overriding the president. At this very moment, the Republicans in the Senate and the White House are conspiring to keep the House of Representatives from reclaiming the war powers that the constitution grants to Congress.

That battle is but the small end of the sword, if you will. The big end is that if we do go to war with Iran, for example, it will be without any congressional input, whatsoever. The latest disaster for the United States will be perpetrated by the executive branch alone, without any accountability. That is the degree to which the decision-making process with regard to war has been usurped by the president.

Of course, saying that decision-making is centralized in the White House is not the entire story. That White House we see today was created by, and takes its marching orders from, a predatory and transnational capitalist state where defense contractors, investment bankers, and hedge fund billionaires call the shots. Then there is big oil, big food, and big energy. Needless to say, having the decision-making so centralized makes it much easier for the big money from these groups to have impact than would be the case if decision-making were spread across the cabinet or across the government. Also, there is no moment in the process when anyone asks what the national interest is, what the long-term implications are.

Pastreich: Let's come back to China for a moment. What are the risks for America here?

Wilkerson: First, let's consider what the role of the United States should be—and, not just about juicy military budgets resulting from the China threat.

These days the United States is just a disruptor in Asia, and an unintelligent disruptor at that. We swing from cooing "I love you, Kim Jong Un" to imposing vicious tariffs on Chinese goods to creating a major embarrassment for Japanese Prime Minister Abe when he tried to help out with Iran.

And most of us were shocked to see Trump mocking how Japanese speak and how Koreans speak. That was the president of the United States! He was not speaking to Prime Minister Abe or to President Moon, but to a racist audience at home and for strictly domestic political purposes.

But to a certain degree the future role of the United States in East Asia will be determined by power dynamics in the region as much as by US policy. Some Americans might want to stay, to be a hegemon in Northeast Asia forever. But that is not a sustainable policy. There is a desperate need for the United States to find a middle ground, a course that preserves some essential American influence within a cooperative framework. The competition with China, and other powers, is going to be substantial at all levels, and simply painting China as a bogeyman is not going to do the trick.

First, we need to go back to good old-fashioned diplomacy. That is more important than any fighter plane or missile. No state is going to fare well in a hot war, or even in a new cold war. We need to use our creativity to shape a culture that supports arms treaties, disarmament, and peace in general—peaceful competition, if you will. And we must build an off-ramp that allows America to dismount the imperial train and steer away from global hegemony and towards global cooperation.

Oddly enough, I think Trump is—very inexpertly, imperfectly, and probably unknowingly—digging out the foundations for such a new collaborative order through his destructive fits. He calls into question the value of NATO, and the so-called deep state is immediately up in arms. So, although Trump may be doing many destructive things, he is also drawing attention to the anachronism that NATO has become post-Cold War. The alliance no longer has any purpose except to seek out trouble "out of area" to justify itself.

We need to have the courage to discuss how we will bring back US troops from the Korean Peninsula, and under what circumstances. We cannot consider that discussion a taboo topic. We also need to use our imagination, and our commitment, to create a regional order that assures the continued security of the Korean Peninsula without that US troop presence.

Let's be honest with ourselves. If the United States wants to maintain its influence in East Asia, its needs plans to bring its troops back from other parts of East Asia, including Japan and particularly Okinawa. We will be much better off if we take the initiative than if we are pushed out by some disaster or another.

And in terms of policy change, I am not just talking about security issues. The United States today is flat-out bankrupt, with a $22 trillion debt. Annual interest payments on that debt added to the annual military budget will zero-out all other discretionary federal spending in less than a decade. We just did something unprecedented: we printed billions of dollars under the Quantitative Easing program with absolutely nothing behind those dollars except the paper and ink on which they were printed.

We have no earthly idea what such profligacy will produce in the future. We have new security challenges like a changing climate and we had better start saving money, and learning to respond to new security challenges, in a manner that does not require such an expensive military instrument.

Pastreich: How can the United States fashion a different strategy for engaging with the world?

Wilkerson: Ambassador Richard Haass threw out the concept of "integration" back in 2001 in his discussions with his Policy Planning staff. He thought that "integration" was the best one-word substitution for "containment." For Haass, integration was a concept that offered an alternative to globalization and its demand for unending expansion and extraction. Haass did not like the concept of globalization, and I think he was right.

Globalization has happened before, in the 1890s, for example. But globalization brings contradictions and tensions that are dangerous. What is going on today goes beyond globalization. What we see happening today is integration: integration of trade, integration of society, integration of culture. That integration is at times mean, disruptive, hateful, and dangerous, but it's happening.

Trade is where we observe the most profound integration. For example, the United States cannot make a sophisticated piece of military equipment any longer without employing foreign components.

But Trump is heading in the opposite direction. He wants to take apart trade agreements and institutions, to disintegrate, not to integrate, trade. And he thinks that somehow the destruction of global institutions will save "white America."

3

The Doomsday Clock Ticks On

Julian Borger

Julian Borger is a British journalist and nonfiction writer who currently serves as the world affairs editor at the Guardian. *He was a correspondent in the US, Eastern Europe, the Middle East, and the Balkans. He is the author of a book on the pursuit and capture of the Balkan war criminals called* The Butcher's Trail.

The Doomsday Clock was a relic of the Cold War that was meant to symbolically depict the "countdown" to imminent nuclear annihilation. It has since expanded to include other factors that destabilize the peace of the planet. In this viewpoint, Borger presents the perspective of the Bulletin of Atomic Scientists, the organization behind the Doomsday Clock, and the reasons they moved the clock forward in 2018. America once again features rather prominently in the rationale, for reasons including the president's relationship with North Korea, the appointment of climate change deniers into the administration, and climate change in general.

The risk to global civilisation is as high today as it has ever been in the face of twin threats, nuclear weapons and climate change, a group of leading scientists has announced, putting a significant share of the blame on the Trump administration.

The Bulletin of the Atomic Scientists moved its symbolic Doomsday Clock forward 30 seconds, to two minutes to midnight, in a reflection of how the scientists view the dangers facing the world.

"'Doomsday Clock' ticked forward 30 seconds to 2 minutes to Midnight," by Julian Borger, Guardian News and Media Limited, January 25, 2018. Reprinted by permission.

The only other time the clock was set so close to catastrophe in its 71-year history was in 1953, after the US and the Soviet Union detonated their first thermonuclear bombs.

In the immediate aftermath of the cold war, the clock was set back to 17 minutes to midnight, but optimism about humanity's future has steadily eroded since then.

"To call the world's nuclear situation dire is to understate the danger and its immediacy," said Rachel Bronson, the bulletin's president and CEO, told journalists in Washington.

In explaining their decision on Thursday, scientists from the bulletin's widely respected science and security board said that they were disturbed by the rising tensions on the Korean peninsula, the increasing emphasis and expenditure on nuclear weapons by major powers, the absence of arms control negotiations around the world, and the wavering political will to combat climate change.

In the year since the hands on the Doomsday Clock were last adjusted, North Korea has carried out its sixth nuclear test, the most powerful to date and almost certainly its first hydrogen bomb. It has also made three successful tests of intercontinental ballistic missiles, the third of which, in November, appeared to be capable of reaching New York or Washington.

At the same time, Trump has engaged in a highly personalised exchange of insults with North Korea's leader, Kim Jong-un. He has threatened "fire and fury" against the nation, and vowed to "totally destroy" if Pyongyang continued to threaten the US American strategic bombers have flown north of the 38th parallel that divides the peninsula, along the North Korean coast.

The bulletin's scientists repeatedly singled out the Trump administration as a major factor behind the increased risks to the planet, pointing out the president's volatility as expressed in his tweets and statements; the inconsistency of the administration's foreign policy; and its apparent disdain for science, reflected in its high-level appointments, which have included climate change deniers.

"Our allies and adversaries alike are being forced [into a] thicket of conflicting policy statements, from a US administration weakened in its roster of foreign policy professionals and unable to develop, coordinate and clearly communicate a coherent foreign—much less nuclear—policy," said Robert Rosner, the chair of the bulletin's science and security board. "This inconsistency constitutes a major challenge for deterrence, alliance management and global stability."

Sharon Squassoni, a professor at George Washington University's institute for international science and technology policy also pointed to Russia's role in heightening tensions. Last year, for instance, it fielded ground-launched cruise missiles, violating the 1987 Intermediate-range Nuclear Forces (INF) treaty.

"Russia has engaged in provocative and illegal behaviours thought to be part of cold war history," Squassoni said.

Some experts argue that the comparison with the height of the cold war was an exaggeration.

"During the height of the cold war there was a nontrivial risk of global nuclear annihilation," Vipin Narang, a North Korea and nuclear expert at the Massachusetts Institute of Technology, wrote in a tweet. "Today, the risk of single use may be higher but it's unlikely to threaten global destruction."

The bulletin scientists said that climate change also weighed heavily in their deliberations. After flattening out for some years, global greenhouse gas emissions have continued to rise and the levels of the polar ice caps are at new lows.

"Here in the US, the incoming President Trump promptly appointed a cadre of avowed climate denialists and quickly started reversing existing climate measures," said Sivan Kartha, a senior scientist at the Stockholm Environmental Institute.

Trump was also criticised for downgrading the science in his administration. Lawrence Krauss, the chair of the bulletin's board of sponsors, said that 2017 marked the first time since the position was created more than a half-century ago that there was no presidential science adviser.

"The White House office of science and technology policy is essentially not staffed," Krauss said. "The official mechanisms to tie public policy to reality are currently absent."

4

Settling the Issue of Israel's Nuclear Ambiguity

Zain Hussain

Zain Hussain was a staff member of BASIC, an independent think tank focused on nuclear disarmament. In 2018, he completed his MA in international politics at the School of Oriental and African Studies (SOAS) in London.

In another corner of the world, Israel's ambiguous nuclear policy has influenced relations in the Middle East for decades. It is a balance of non-committal non-denials and controlled leaks that are meant to disquiet other countries in the region, a strategy referred to by the Hebrew term amimut. *Zain elaborates this situation with great detail, tying his arguments closely to the history of the region while depicting the complicated web of information and precedent that informs international relations and policy.*

The Israeli policy of nuclear ambiguity is perhaps one of the most controversial nuclear policies today, and is the subject of some criticism by other states in the Middle East and nuclear disarmament activists.

The history of Israel's nuclear weapons programme began at the time of David Ben Gurion's period in office as Prime Minister of the State of Israel. Ben Gurion expressed the idea that nuclear weapons could act as a deterrent preventing other states in the region from

"Why the Israeli Policy of Nuclear Ambiguity Is Harmful for Prospects of a WMD Free Zone in the Middle East," by Zain Hussain, BASIC, June 21, 2019. Reprinted by permission.

taking steps to destroy the Jewish State. The French were heavily involved in Israel's nuclear programme in its first stages.

Israel started producing heavy water in 1953. France agreed to supply an 18 Megawatt research reactor but then promised to build a 24 MWt reactor and a chemical reprocessing plant instead after the Suez Crisis. The plant was constructed in Dimona in secret, without IAEA safeguards. To help with the Israeli nuclear programme, Britain sold lithium-6, beryllium and 20 tonnes of heavy water to Israel between 1959 and 1960.

The French role in Israel's nuclear weapons programme was deeply duplicitous, and formed the foundations of the policy of ambiguity. France provided Israel with highly sensitive nuclear weapons capabilities, including a plutonium reprocessing facility, and yet required Israel to promise in 1960 that it would never produce nuclear weapons, reprocess plutonium, publicly announce the existence of its reactor, or complete the reactor's construction without French assistance. The cooling system in the Dimona plant was three times larger than was necessary for civil purposes and Israel further enlarged its capacity later.

This assistance was not a one-way engagement. Israeli scientists actively helped in the French nuclear weapons programme when it began in the 1950s, with their nuclear expertise and their participation in bomb tests in Algeria in the early 1960s. According to John Steinbach, the Israeli nuclear programme, "should be understood largely as an extension of this early collaboration."

The Israeli nuclear weapons programme was seen by its architects as a way to achieve self reliance in terms of security. In the early days of the state of Israel, still recovering from the trauma of the holocaust and with an influential narrative of Israel being the salvation for the Jewish people, nuclear deterrence was seen as the ultimate means of ensuring the protection of the Jewish state. Ofer Israeli quotes from Ernst David Bergmann, one of the people involved in the nuclear programme, as saying, "the state of Israel needs a defence research programme of its own, so that we shall never again be as a herd led to the slaughter."

During the 1950s, Israel permitted a brief assessment of the facility at Dimona by the United States but it has not allowed other international inspections of the facility since. There are believed to be several hidden underground levels in the facility, and security has always been tight in the area surrounding the Dimona plant.

Israel has been developing its weapons delivery systems and platforms since the 1960s. These include the F15, F15I and F16 aircraft, Jericho ballistic missiles and Dolphin class submarines provided by the Germans, carrying nuclear-tipped cruise missiles.

The Israeli policy of ambiguity (Amimut) was viewed as a way to keep Israel and its nuclear programme safe as Israel's allies were seen as unreliable. According to the policy, Israel neither officially confirms nor denies that it has nuclear weapons.

There are two elements of Amimut, as Israeli notes:

> *(1) keeping its nuclear enterprise secret, meaning not testing or announcing it has nuclear weapons, and at the same time (2) bolstering its nuclear image through leaks, statements, and rumours, as well as publishing indirect evidence of its existing nuclear capabilities.*

As Zeev Maoz points out, "through a series of leaks and veiled statements, the spread of rumours, and other political actions (e.g., refusal to sign the 1968 Nuclear Non Proliferation Treaty, or NPT), Israel would bolster its nuclear image—an image comprising indirect evidence of an existing nuclear capability and hints of a deterrence doctrine."

This combination of opacity with leaking and suggestion was intended to deliver a deterrent effect while also avoiding or minimising the short and long term ramifications of having an open nuclear weapon monopoly in the region. Maoz also points out that the nuclear weapon programme is a "samson option," the idea that nuclear weapons would be used as a last resort suicide decision.

As such, Israel is able to continue its nuclear weapons programme while retaining relative quiet on the issue in the international sphere, and with few boundaries on what it can do, while continuing to maintain close ties with the United States and other Western nations that profess commitment to non proliferation, which severely punish other states for acquiring sensitive technologies while protecting Israel's position.

Proponents of the ambiguity policy have argued that it has ensured relative security for Israel and that Israel has not been attacked collectively by Arab states. Maoz points out that there has been no evidence of any such intention among Arab neighbours since the Israeli nuclear programme kicked off in the 1960s, but there have been two instances of Arab states forming temporary coalitions to target Israel for partial temporary territorial gain/ reclaim. Prior to 1967, open willingness by Arab states to destroy Israel was common. Such expressions are no longer commonly made by the vast majority of regional states. However, whether Israel's nuclear weapons played any role in this situation is a matter of conjecture. In any case, the goal of retaking Israeli occupied Palestine seems to have been a greater motive to target Israel instead of the very destruction of the state of Israel. This can be seen, for example, in the Arab attempt to reoccupy land taken over by Israel in 1967.

Zeev Maoz, after examining the Israeli policy of nuclear ambiguity, its effectiveness, Israeli public opinion on the issue, and whether or not the nuclear programme itself is what has deterred an all-out Arab attack to annihilate Israel, concludes a number of important insights. Firstly, there is no direct proof that Israel's nuclear policy has provided an effective deterrent against a collective Arab attack on Israel. Secondly, there is no evidence that, when there were attacks on Israel, Israel's nuclear policy in any way affected Arab operational plans. Thirdly, there is no evidence that directly links Israel's nuclear weapons' capability with the willingness of Arab states and Palestinians to negotiate with Israel.

In light of this evidence, Israel's nuclear programme, contrary to what Israeli strategists and academics have claimed, has not contributed to Israel's security in any meaningful way. Maoz's conclusions also show the inherent contradictions in the policy.

In response to such criticism, other authors, academics and policy thinkers have explained their reasons for Israel's continual need for nuclear weapons and its ambiguity policy. Louis Rene Beres has responded directly to Maoz. To him, the Arab states cannot be trusted to uphold peace agreements with Israel. He also believes that, given the slightest chance, Arab countries would attack Israel. He also points to present cases of Middle Eastern Countries, such as Iran, calling for the destruction of Israel.

He argues that, even if other countries in the Middle East were to sign up to a WMD Free Zone in the Middle East, or sign disarmament agreements in Israel, verification of compliance in these matters would be incredibly difficult. For Beres, the problem is not so much with nuclear weapons as it is with what he perceives as an Arab-Iranian commitment to destroy Israel. This commitment means that the "peace plan" is a futile attempt at peace with actors which want nothing less than Israel's destruction. At least one Arab country that has signed peace agreements with Israel, according to Beres, is "effectively at war" with it. With nuclear weapons, Israel can deter strategic conventional attacks by these states. They could also target hard state targets that threaten Israel's existence through non nuclear preemptive strikes, which would otherwise look like a call to war, since there would be no context of a credible potential retaliation threat from Israel.

Beres argues further that Israel's nuclear amimut policy may need to be reviewed and replaced by a policy of more transparent disclosure in the future, for the purpose of highlighting to enemy states and forces the capabilities that Israel has and to let them know that Israel is willing to use them in response to some strategic first-strike attacks… a message supported by the modernisation of Israel's nuclear weapon systems. It was important to elucidate Beres' comments because many of the arguments he raises are accepted as conventional wisdom among those who support Israel's nuclear programme.

Maoz has responded to many of Beres's assertions and grievances. While Beres asserts that Israeli possession of nuclear weapons is necessary to safeguard Israel from a state of catastrophic war, there is no evidence that the Arab states have invested in such a war, it has not deterred the Arab states from forming coalitions to attack Israel in 1967 and 1973, and there is no evidence that nuclear weapons have inclined the Arab states more towards or against peace. However, there may be evidence that Israel's nuclear weapons programme could have increased the non conventional arms race in the region. Maoz points out the effects that Israel's nuclear programme may have had on Iraq's WMD programme, and in Egypt and Syria pursuing and developing chemical weapons, biological weapons, and surface to surface missiles.

Maoz questions Beres' assumptions about Arab states and particularly their supposed lack of willingness to have peace with Israel. Maoz refers to a letter written by Yasir Arafat in 1988 for President Clinton, in which he wrote that, "the Palestine National Council's resolution is a comprehensive amendment of the Covenant. All of the provisions of the Covenant which are inconsistent with the PLO commitment to recognize and live in peace side by side with Israel are no longer in effect….I can assure you on behalf of the PLO and the Palestinian Authority that all the provisions of the Covenant that were inconsistent with the commitments of September 9/10, 1993 to Prime Minister Rabin, have been nullified." He also argues that, even if the PA were not to stand behind this, and were to be committed to Israel's destruction, nuclear weapons would not deter them.

Maoz points out that Egypt has not violated its peace treaty with Israel, even when Israel launched an unprovoked attack on Syria and Lebanon in 1982. Similarly, when its forces were attacked by Israeli forces, Syria did not violate its May 1974 agreement with Israel. In 2000, when the al-Aqsa intifada started, Syria, Jordan and Egypt did not violate their treaty agreements.

After its 1979 peace treaty with Israel, Egypt reduced its defense budget, from a height of 22 percent in 1974 to 2.75 percent in 2002. In 2002, Syria's defence budget was roughly 6.7 percent of its GDP. By contrast, Israel, at the time Maoz was writing in 2004, had a defense burden approaching 10 percent of a much larger GDP, whilst also receiving substantial military assistance from the United States. Maoz continues to note:

> *The combined defense expenditures of Egypt, Syria, Jordan and Lebanon (the four contiguous states to Israel), amount only to 58 percent of Israel's defense expenditures. Coupled with Israeli nuclear weapons, if anyone should be more concerned about security, it is the leaders of these Arab states. These figures also suggest that Israeli weapons did not play an important role in reducing its defense burden.*

At the same time, Israel's policy of amimut may well have done more harm than good. It may have encouraged other states in the region to increase their WMD capacity. The policy both seeks to prevent Israel from being held accountable for its nuclear weapons programme, while also making it clear through leaks (intentional and not) and behaviour that it has one, for deterrence purposes. Even some proponents of the nuclear weapons programme, such as Beres, have argued that the policy should be jettisoned in favour of more open disclosure for deterrence purposes.

Israel has not permitted international inspection of its sensitive nuclear facilities. Its unwillingness to be held accountable to the international community deepens mistrust in the region towards Israel.

Israeli Amimut and a WMD Free Zone in the Middle East

Israel's opacity over its nuclear weapons possession has been a principal hindrance to the establishment of a WMD Free Zone in the Middle East. Yet, it appears that for many states within the international community Israel's nuclear possession is more acceptable than other states having any ambiguity in their nuclear capability. This explicit double standard deepens the sense of injustice within the region, further driving hostility to Israel, and undermining the ability of much of the international community to play the role of honest broker.

Moreover, due to the nature of nuclear amimut, Israel cannot have any sort of declaratory policy. It cannot clearly signal the purpose of its nuclear weapons and cannot communicate any limitations on its possible use of its nuclear weapons. It is, in other words, an extreme position of complete ambiguity, with damaging impacts on the security of other states, and to diplomatic attempts to limit damage to the global non-proliferation regime. Israel has already said that it would not introduce nuclear weapons to the region, but has clearly broken this promise.

Its possession without restraint leaves open the suspicion that Israel is able to engage in aggressive military action in the region safe in the knowledge that its nuclear monopoly prevents assertive reaction.

Israel has frequently declared its official support for a WMD Free Zone in the Middle East at UN meetings, but has also argued that such a zone could only be achieved once there was peace and mutual recognition within the region. Arab states see this as a stalling tactic, and could imply some kind of justification for Israel's secret nuclear arsenal. There have been a number of proposals to consider the Zone in parallel with a wider regional security dialogue, but these have yet to get anywhere. If there is to be any progress, Israel would do well to consider how its policy of Amimut undermines its own long-term security as well as prospects of a WMD Free Zone in the Middle East.

5

Defusing Nuclear Tension in Iran

Noah Weisbord

Noah Weisbord is an associate professor at Queen's University in Ontario, Canada. His research focuses on the role of criminal law in managing, reflecting, or exacerbating intergroup conflict. His written work has appeared in the Harvard International Law Journal, *the* New York Times, *and the* National Post.

America-Iran relations have significantly deteriorated since the initial publication of this piece in June 2019, but it reflects and expresses the many anxieties that plague the current discourse on Iran. Indeed, the viewpoint author at one point likens the situation to the lead-up to World War I. At the center of this issue are Iran's nuclear program and the attempted or reneged deals that follow it. This also presents a troubled front for the Trump administration's foreign policy.

Iran's Revolutionary Guard Corps shot down a sophisticated US surveillance drone with a surface-to-air missile on June 20th. The US and Iran disagree about whether the drone was in Iranian or international airspace.

The next day, President Trump warned that American forces were "cocked and loaded" to strike three targets in Iran but that he had called off the strikes ten minutes before they were launched.

"What Does the Trump Administration Want from Iran?" by Noah Weisbord, The Conversation, June 13, 2019. https://theconversation.com/what-does-the-trump-administration-want-from-iran-117797.

The incident came after two oil tankers were attacked on June 13 off the coast of Oman, forcing the crew members of one burning ship to flee.

It was the latest in a series of assaults on tankers transporting oil through the Gulf. In May, Saudi, Norwegian and Emirati oil tankers were attacked off the coast of the United Arab Emirates, causing damage but no casualties. The attacks have gone unclaimed, so the perpetrator is unknown—at least publicly.

US ally Saudi Arabia, Iran's regional rival, blamed the Iranian government and called the May attacks "naked aggression." Saudi King Salman asked the international community to "use all means" to punish Iran.

US national security adviser John Bolton, who has called for bombing Iran to cripple its nuclear program, has maintained that Iran is "almost certainly" responsible for the attacks. In May Bolton announced the deployment to the Persian Gulf of a carrier strike group and a nuclear-capable bomber task force, America's most formidable military assets.

The purpose: "to send a clear and unmistakable message" to Iran.

What Does the US Want?

But the White House is squabbling over its objectives, which are far from clear. Trump administration officials do not seem to agree whether the US wants behavior change or regime change. Should the US use diplomacy or force? Are frustrated Iranians or frustrated Americans the target of this military deployment?

President Trump told U.K. television host Piers Morgan that military options are on the table but, "I'd much rather talk."

According to Washington Post columnist David Ignatius, President Trump "wants to sound tough (popular) so long as it doesn't get him into a war (unpopular)." President Trump "doesn't want to go to war with Iran," retired General David Petraeus told ABC News.

As a scholar who has studied the onset of a number of wars, I believe these commentators underestimate the influence of shrewd warmongers like Bolton. They also fail to credit how quickly a trivial confrontation between industrialized forces can change a leader's calculus and drag the great powers and their allies into war.

The showdown in the Persian Gulf is not like the US and the Soviet Union incrementally adjusting the balance of power, as they did during the Cold War.

Mixed signals, bad timing and this kind of uncalibrated brinksmanship is how World War I began and spiraled out of control. It has brought the US closer to the next Middle East war.

Up to the Edge

Iran brokered a deal with the US, the EU, Russia, China and Germany in 2015 to curtail its nuclear program in exchange for sanctions relief.

The current standoff began in May 2018 when President Trump reneged on the deal and later implemented a new "maximum pressure" campaign against Iran, which included economic sanctions punishing countries purchasing Iranian oil.

The U.K., France, China, Russia and Germany pledged to abide by the terms of the deal. Nevertheless, US sanctions against Iranian industry at a time when Iran was complying with the deal are collapsing the Iranian economy.

The White House claims its "maximum pressure" policy is working—that Iran is cutting aid to malevolent allies and proxies in the region, including Syrian President Bashar al-Assad, Hezbollah and Hamas.

US Secretary of State Mike Pompeo maintains, without evidence or a tangible timeline, that grueling economic conditions created by the US will turn frustrated Iranians against their leaders, provoking regime change.

That idea seems to me to be magical thinking. US belligerence, especially when it has been rejected by the broader international community—as it is now by parties to the 2015 nuclear deal—is more likely to turn Iranians against the US, polarize US allies and strengthen Iran's hardliners.

Cosmopolitan Iranian youth, for example, who are the best hope for peace with the US, are the most likely group to turn against their government—but not if the Trump administration strangles their economy and threatens to invade their country.

Limited Choices

In the meantime, Iran's economic troubles are narrowing its options.

According to the International Atomic Energy Agency, Iran has accelerated uranium enrichment and intends to quadruple production, in violation of the nuclear deal. Attacks on US forces or allies, including Israel, are becoming increasingly appealing to Iranian leaders to give Iran some leverage against the US.

The prospect of economic collapse under draconian sanctions by the US also provokes Iran's leaders to instigate a confrontation sooner rather than later, while its military and proxies are strong. Iranian President Hassan Rouhani has given Germany, the U.K., France, China and Russia 60 days to honor their promise to buttress Iranian energy and banking sectors before taking additional steps to withdraw from the nuclear deal.

Iran's economic and military weakness also encourages its leadership to cooperate more closely with America's foreign adversaries, including Russia, despite Iran's aversion to ceding precious influence in the region.

If the Iran-Russia relationship tightens, it will result in even greater tension with the US. Increased Iranian-Russian cooperation is also an invitation to US leaders to strike before US troops find themselves facing an emboldened Iranian military reinforced with Russian equipment and know-how.

With each day of US sanctions, Iran's leaders become increasingly desperate, with diminished leverage should the two countries face off on the battlefield or at the negotiating table.

Defusing the Tension

With tensions rising, the US has sent an additional 1,500 troops to the Middle East. President Trump plans to send 1,000 more. Iran's 60-day ultimatum to parties to the nuclear deal expires in early July.

According to Supreme Leader Ayatollah Khamenei, "Negotiation has no benefit and carries harm."

Iran experts Colin Kahl and Jon Wolfsthal warn, "Bolton's preferences, not Trump's, are winning out."

There is still time for President Trump to extract the US from this dangerous standoff that he allowed to escalate.

Some hope lies in Japanese Prime Minister Shinzo Abe.

Japan, which is not party to the 2015 nuclear deal, is a major purchaser of Iranian oil and Abe is perceived to be a neutral broker.

Abe visited Iran last week—the first Japanese leader to do so in four decades—and met with Supreme Leader Ayatollah Khamenei and Rouhani to discuss the standoff. But it is unclear what Abe accomplished.

A potential solution lies in intense, nuanced diplomacy where the US, building on the 2015 nuclear deal, trades sanction relief for slightly tougher limits on Iran's nuclear program.

This includes renegotiating the restrictions on Iran's centrifuges, mandatory international inspections, and its accumulation of nuclear material. A slightly modified nuclear deal like Trump's slightly modified trade agreement with Canada and Mexico, can be recast as victory by all.

Trump emerges as peacemaker and potential contender for the Nobel Prize. Iran's leaders can then right their economy.

Trump's winning outcome, however, is not the outcome Bolton has long advocated.

For decades, Bolton has publicly agitated for preventive strikes against Iraq, North Korea and Iran. Only grudgingly, perhaps for fear of losing his job, has Bolton acquiesced to a policy of behavior change over regime change.

This is the price Bolton pays to remain the president's national security adviser—filterer of Trump's intelligence reports, first one in and last one out of the room whenever the president is discussing matters of war and peace.

If Abe fails, the current Iran crisis may yet become the culmination of Bolton's lifelong ambition. When new explosions rock the Persian Gulf, US troops are injured or killed by Iranian proxies in Iraq, or Iranian-made drones pepper the Saudi skies, will President Trump resist the urge to escalate?

6

The Resurgence of Fascism and Nuclear Armament

Louie Dean Valencia-García

Dr. Louie Dean Valencia-García is a senior fellow at the Centre for Analysis of the Radical Right and assistant professor of digital history at Texas State University. He is the author of Antiauthoritarian Youth Culture in Francoist Spain: Clashing with Fascism *and a research editor for* EuropeNow, *the journal of the Council for European Studies at Columbia University.*

Valencia-García points out a troubling trend in modern journalism—that fascist and Nazi behavior is rarely called out as such by the media. In this viewpoint, Valencia-García proposes that journalists reframe their narratives and call a spade a spade. This may seem a question of semantics, but—according to the author—the choice of language matters. Historically, fascist regimes would use a population's anxiety and fear of others to justify large-scale violence against them. A modern resurgence of fascism would likely follow the pattern, but we have not yet seen a nuclear fascist state.

It's time we said it. We are living in a world in which fascism has not only become mainstream, but it is at war with our democratic institutions—from the inside. In the aftermath of the Holocaust, scholars and journalists have consistently tried to be careful about labeling something "fascist." Mussolini's fascist

"Trump and the Global Resurgence of Fascism," by Louie Dean Valencia-García, Rantt Media Inc., June 18, 2019. Reprinted by permission.

movement indeed was part of a particular historical moment and should be thought that way. Nazism was a gross and depraved ideology of its time. To differentiate then and now we have come up with terms like "neo-Nazi," "far-right," etc. In the past, I have even advocated to use terms like "fascistic" and to identify "fascist tendencies" to describe contemporary radical right ideologies.

During a live stream this week, New York Representative Alexandria Ocasio-Cortez rightly identified the immigrant detention centers across the United States as "concentration camps" and this presidency as "fascist." Of course, right-wing commentators feel the need to reject this uncomfortable truth—to say such a comparison demeans the memory of the Holocaust. But does it really?

We are living in a world where liberalism, capitalism, communism, anarchism, socialism, and authoritarianism all co-exist. With multitudes of variation, all of these ideas have survived their initial inceptions and definitions for at least a century, if not more. If these "-isms" can endure and adapt to changing times, then why hasn't fascism? The truth of the matter is that it has. The left has avoided labeling anything as fascist, perhaps out of respect for the tragedy of what the Holocaust was or because fascism became the unnameable evil. On the right, well, all liberals are fascists and advocates for women's rights are Feminazis.

Perhaps we decided not to say the f-word because we thought by saying it, we would call it into being—like Voldemort. However, in not explicitly saying something was fascist, we missed the opportunity to both teach what fascism means and, more dangerously, gave ethno-nationalist movements and activists cover—and the ability to rebrand themselves.

Meanwhile, fascists were attempting to find names that either sound innocuous or weirdly hip. Vice co-founder Gavin McInnes, once a veritable Brooklyn hipster, has founded a far-right group known as the "Proud Boys" which is particularly concerned about the status of "western civilization." "White nationalist" Richard Spencer is the founder of the "Alt-Right," calls himself an "Identitarian," enjoys reading the works of the "New Right," and runs the "National Policy Institute." The once-fringe French "Front National" is now "National Rally." The transnational youth group "Generation Identity" now prefers sleek neutral blues and white colors to the more ominous yellow and black color scheme when they rent helicopters and boats to search the mountains and the Mediterranean for refugees—to return them to their homelands.

The preppy American branch of the youth Identitarian movement recently changed its name from "Identity Evropa" to the "American Identity Movement." Pointedly, GQ has even said "there's nothing controversial" about calling US president Donald Trump's senior policy advisor, Stephen Miller, a white nationalist. Miller even organized with Spencer at Duke University, where Spencer says he mentored Miller. Of course, some, like Russian ideologue Alexander Dugin, are calling their ideologies a new political theory altogether. This is late fascism.

Why This Is Modern Fascism

We call these movements and people "white nationalist," "white supremacist," "far-right" and "radical right"—which they are. These subcategories are clarifying to better understand particularity. However, they all fall under the larger umbrella of fascism. More to the point, they are "late fascist" movements—postwar fascism that has incorporated postmodern relativism, appropriated leftist discourse, and implemented irony and trendy aesthetics to disguise putrid fascist ideology that seemingly had been rejected writ-large after the Holocaust.

These movements decry the fall of western civilization, and see themselves in a Crusade against Islam, immigrants, globalism and so-called "identity politics" and "multiculturalism." They believe in a conspiracy known as "the great replacement"—labeling it "white genocide." All of this is thinly-veiled coded language to say they don't want people of color, Jews, Muslims, women and queer people to find equality, because they are afraid of losing power. They dislike global capitalism because they see it as a Jewish conspiracy, not because of the actual failings of late capitalism as an economic model.

The United States and European media resist calling Donald Trump fascist, explicitly: "Mr Trump is not a fascist, if by that you mean a successor to Mussolini or Hitler." Of course, that isn't the definition of fascism—Hitler and Mussolini were two early twentieth century manifestations of fascism. Curiously, major US and European news sources frequently describe politicians in Europe as "far-right," but despite Trump calling himself a nationalist, recognizing the disfavor of that term and advocating for its return, by and large most media exculpates Trump from being called radical right, or fascist for that matter, suggesting he merely confuses nationalism and patriotism.

This refusal to label Trump, or the likes of Steve Bannon, Nigel Farage and Boris Johnson, as part of a late fascist wave is, in fact, enabling and also a potential sign that we don't want to admit that at least one branch of the United States government has fallen into fascist ideology. There is a cognitive dissonance in saying American or European democracies have democratically become fascist.

Recently, Ocasio-Cortez questioned FBI Assistant Director for Counterterrorism Michael McGarrity, eliciting him to specifically state that the under current federal law the US Congress did not categorize white nationalism as domestic terrorism. She argued we have seen "white supremacist attacks that were clearly domestic terrorism." Despite this assertion, ABC News reporter Mike Levine claimed, "Ocasio-Cortez appeared to be confusing two different types of FBI cases," insisting "None of the perpetrators in those ISIS-inspired cases was designated or charged as a 'domestic terrorist.' Instead, they were each designated and charged as a 'homegrown violent extremist,' which may sound like a 'domestic terrorist' but is actually quite different, at least to the FBI."

Levine simply did not understand that what Ocasio-Cortez was arguing for is precisely a change in the way the category of "domestic terrorism" is defined. As a representative, it is her job to question and challenge existing laws and their definitions and to propose more effective laws. In fact, what Ocasio-Cortez elucidates is that her peers in Congress need to change the category of what is defined as terrorism. Levine incorrectly portrayed Ocasio-Cortez as not understanding those categories when, in fact, she was pointing out the very need for a change in categories. Understanding how we define categories is essential to most effectively combat fascism.

Jason Stanley, author of *How Fascism Works: The Politics of Us and Them,* has stated, "The question—'Is Trump a fascist?'— is to me a less interesting and less relevant question than 'why Trump's message resonated so much that he won in 2016, and why he may well win again.'" Another relevant question might be: if President Trump's attacks on the press, persecuting ethnic and religious minorities, undermining of the rule of law, and other undemocratic behavior isn't fascism, then what is? To be sure, passing the day arguing point by point whether or not Trump is a fascist is banal. What is important is that we understand why Trump, and others like him, won and continue to make strides forward.

To understand this, we have to think of it not as a political trend, but as part of what is clearly becoming a part of an emerging ideology that can and should be described as late fascism—a fascism for our current era. Stanley argues:

> *The Trump presidency is a violent response to more than two centuries of struggle for human rights and dignity. When Trump speaks of making America great again, we know what many of his most passionate supporters hear. They want white supremacy to be not just the reality, but the official policy.*

One of the major constitutive factors of fascism is, of course, its willingness to engage in violence. At least one historian, Timothy Snyder, has called Trump and his tactics fascist. Historians often look for violence as a defining characteristic of fascism. Are immigrant concentration camps not enough? What about violent domestic terrorism by the radical right? What about attacks on black churches, Jewish temples and Muslim mosques in the US and abroad? The German government even cautioned Jews about wearing the kippah, or skullcap, in the country because of rising anti-Semitism. And what about unpunished police violence in the US against people of color? There are continual legal attacks on women and queer people. Trump has promised beginning next week "ICE will begin the process of removing… millions of illegal aliens"—what rings too much of a Kristallnacht-level event, when Hitler's SA forces arrested some 30,000 Jews, taking them to concentration camps. Trump's statement all but guarantees the harassment of people of color across the United States.

Fascism, in all its ugliness, is all around us—and those with some modicum of distance—privilege—can still go to our local Starbucks and participate in a capitalist economy without worry. Ideologies and economic systems aren't exclusive—they can, and do, co-exist and overlap. We are living in a world where we are constantly clashing with fascism.

Cas Mudde rightly argues in the wake of the recent European elections that "populist radical right, in particular, has become mainstreamed and normalized." Mudde continues, "We find it normal that a neo-Nazi party is the third biggest party in a member state, that a populist radical right wins more than half of the vote in non-democratic elections, and that the populist radical right is the biggest party in several EU member states." Despite this, Deutsche Welle reports "No new dawn for far right in European election."

On the contrary, the election results show considerable normalization of fascism and its stronghold on normal politics. Marine Le Pen's National Rally party actually won more votes than Emmanuel Macron's party coalition. Matteo Salvini's Northern League had a victory with 34% of the vote. Viktor Orbán in Hungry had 52% of the vote. The Brexit Party had 30% of the vote. In Spain, already, the Vox party had won 24 parliamentary seats in the Spanish elections in April—this problem is not going away until we can at least name it.

Sometimes, if you give the monster under the bed a name, it doesn't make it go away, but it at least lets us know what you are dealing with and how you can confront it. The problem is fascism taking hold of national governments and politics, and we actually do know how to deal with it. First, we need to change the narrative and call it by its name.

7

Fear of Nuclear Weapons Caused the War in Iraq

Ahsan I. Butt

Ahsan I. Butt is an associate professor at the Schar School of Policy and Government at George Mason University in Virginia and a nonresident fellow at the Stimson Center. He is the author of Secession and Security: Explaining State Strategy Against Separatists.

Nuclear weapons and their destructive capability are rightfully feared, but as this viewpoint indicates, it is generally the fear and anxiety that it evokes that drives policy rather than their outright use. Butt re-examines former president George W. Bush's war with Iraq in this light—a war that initially was justified under the guise of Iraq's possession of weapons of mass destruction (WMD). History has since proven this wrong, and unfortunately, history may repeat itself with the current US-Iran conflict.

Sixteen years after the United States invaded Iraq and left a trail of destruction and chaos in the country and the region, one aspect of the war remains criminally underexamined: why was it fought in the first place? What did the Bush administration hope to get out of the war?

The official, and widely-accepted, story remains that Washington was motivated by Saddam Hussein's weapons of mass destruction (WMD) programme. His nuclear capabilities,

"Why Did Bush Go to War in Iraq?" by Ahsan I. Butt, Al Jazeera Media Network, March 20, 2019. Reprinted by permission.

especially, were deemed sufficiently alarming to incite the war. As then US Secretary of State Condoleezza Rice said, "We do not want the smoking gun to be a mushroom cloud."

Despite Saddam not having an active WMD programme, this explanation has found support among some International Relations scholars, who say that while the Bush administration was wrong about Saddam's WMD capabilities, it was sincerely wrong. Intelligence is a complicated, murky enterprise, the argument goes, and given the foreboding shadow of the 9/11 attacks, the US government reasonably, if tragically, misread the evidence on the dangers Saddam posed.

There is a major problem with this thesis: there is no evidence for it, beyond the words of the Bush officials themselves. And since we know the administration was engaged in a widespread campaign of deception and propaganda in the run-up to the Iraq war, there is little reason to believe them.

My investigation into the causes of the war finds that it had little to do with fear of WMDs—or other purported goals, such as a desire to "spread democracy" or satisfy the oil or Israel lobbies. Rather, the Bush administration invaded Iraq for its demonstration effect.

A quick and decisive victory in the heart of the Arab world would send a message to all countries, especially to recalcitrant regimes such as Syria, Libya, Iran, or North Korea, that American hegemony was here to stay. Put simply, the Iraq war was motivated by a desire to (re)establish American standing as the world's leading power.

Indeed, even before 9/11, then-Secretary of Defense Donald Rumsfeld saw Iraq through the prism of status and reputation, variously arguing in February and July 2001 that ousting Saddam would "enhance US credibility and influence throughout the region" and "demonstrate what US policy is all about."

These hypotheticals were catalysed into reality by September 11, when symbols of American military and economic dominance were destroyed. Driven by humiliation, the Bush administration felt that the US needed to reassert its position as an unchallengeable hegemon.

The only way to send a message so menacing was a swashbuckling victory in war. Crucially, however, Afghanistan was not enough: it was simply too weak a state. As prison bullies know, a fearsome reputation is not acquired by beating up the weakest in the yard. Or as Rumsfeld put it on the evening of 9/11, "We need to bomb something else to prove that we're, you know, big and strong and not going to be pushed around by these kinds of attacks."

Moreover, Afghanistan was a "fair" war, a tit-for-tat response to the Taliban's provision of sanctuary to al-Qaeda's leadership. Rumsfeld, Deputy Secretary of Defense Paul Wolfowitz, and Under Secretary of Defense for Policy Douglas Feith considered restricting retaliation to Afghanistan dangerously "limited," "meager," and "narrow." Doing so, they alleged, "may be perceived as a sign of weakness rather than strength" and prove to "embolden rather than discourage regimes" opposed to the US. They knew that sending a message of unbridled hegemony entailed a disproportionate response to 9/11, one that had to extend beyond Afghanistan.

Iraq fit the bill both because it was more powerful than Afghanistan and because it had been in neoconservative crosshairs since George HW Bush declined to press on to Baghdad in 1991. A regime remaining defiant despite a military defeat was barely tolerable before 9/11. Afterwards, however, it became untenable.

That Iraq was attacked for its demonstration effect is attested to by several sources, not least the principals themselves—in private. A senior administration official told a reporter, off the record, that "Iraq is not just about Iraq," rather "it was of a type," including Iran, Syria, and North Korea.

In a memo issued on September 30, 2001, Rumsfeld advised Bush that "the USG [US government] should envision a goal along these lines: New regimes in Afghanistan and another key State [or two] that supports terrorism [to strengthen political and military efforts to change policies elsewhere]."

Feith wrote to Rumsfeld in October 2001 that action against Iraq would make it easier to "confront—politically, militarily, or otherwise" Libya and Syria. As for then-Vice President Dick Cheney, one close adviser revealed that his thinking behind the war was to show: "We are able and willing to strike at someone. That sends a very powerful message."

In a 2002 column, Jonah Goldberg coined the "Ledeen Doctrine," named after neoconservative historian Michael Ledeen. The "doctrine" states: "Every ten years or so, the United States needs to pick up some small crappy little country and throw it against the wall, just to show the world we mean business."

It may be discomfiting to Americans to say nothing of millions of Iraqis that the Bush administration spent their blood and treasure for a war inspired by the Ledeen Doctrine. Did the US really start a war—one that cost trillions of dollars, killed hundreds of thousands of Iraqis, destabilised the region, and helped create the Islamic State of Iraq and the Levant (ISIL)—just to prove a point?

More uncomfortable still is that the Bush administration used WMDs as a cover, with equal parts fearmongering and strategic misrepresentation—lying—to exact the desired political effect. Indeed, some US economists consider the notion that the Bush administration deliberately misled the country and the globe into war in Iraq to be a "conspiracy theory," on par with beliefs that President Barack Obama was born outside the US or that the Holocaust did not occur.

But this, sadly, is no conspiracy theory. Even Bush officials have sometimes dropped their guard. Feith confessed in 2006 that "the rationale for the war didn't hinge on the details of this intelligence even though the details of the intelligence at times became elements of the public presentation."

That the administration used the fear of WMDs and terrorism to fight a war for hegemony should be acknowledged by an

American political establishment eager to rehabilitate George W Bush amid the rule of Donald Trump, not least because John Bolton, Trump's national security adviser, seems eager to employ similar methods to similar ends in Iran.

8

Moving Toward a WMD-Free Middle East

Pierre Goldschmidt

Pierre Goldschmidt is a Belgian nuclear scientist who served as the deputy director general and head of safeguards at the International Atomic Energy Agency until 2005. He then became a nonresident senior associate at the Carnegie Endowment for International Peace until the end of 2017.

Every corner of the Middle East is increasingly destabilized and fraught with war and the issue of destructive weaponry—be it conventional guns, chemical weapons, or nuclear weapons. American intervention played no small role in creating this hotbed, but what's the next step forward? Goldschmidt outlines a slow and bureaucratic plan that invites all parties to the table and brings up key challenges to the goal of a demilitarized zone in the Middle East.

Initiatives taken in favor of global nuclear disarmament deserve the full support of the international community, although actually achieving a world without nuclear weapons will require many incremental steps over an extended period of time.

The creation of a weapons of mass destruction-free zone (WMDFZ) in the Middle East remains an oft-discussed idea when considering steps toward a world free of nuclear weapons.[1] Nowhere is such a zone needed more than in the Middle East. However, the notable absence of favorable conditions presents significant

"A Realistic Approach Toward a Middle East Free of WMD," by Pierre Goldschmidt, Carnegie Endowment for International Peace, July 7, 2016. Reprinted by permission.

challenges in reaching this goal. In fact, no WMDFZ or nuclear-weapon-free zone (NWFZ) has ever been established among states at war, as has formally been the case between Israel and Syria since Israel's creation in 1948. Nor has one ever been established between states that do not officially recognize the existence of a state in their region as a political entity and thus share no diplomatic relations, as is the case with many states in the region, including Iran, toward Israel.

The political circumstances that characterize the Middle East therefore render a WMDFZ unlikely in the foreseeable future. In fact, as experience over the past twenty years has demonstrated, insisting on the establishment of such a zone at once, without first implementing confidence-building measures, is not only unrealistic but counterproductive.

Most states in the Middle East have ratified both the Chemical Weapons Convention (CWC) and the Biological Weapons Convention (BWC). Key holdouts include Israel (which has signed but not ratified the CWC and has not signed the BWC) and Egypt (which has not signed the CWC, and has signed but not ratified the BWC). Meanwhile, after using chemical weapons and coming under the threat of US airstrikes, Syria ratified the CWC in October 2013. It has also signed but not ratified the BWC.

Even after all states in the region have ratified both treaties, more work will still be needed to verifiably eliminate biological and chemical weapons; the BWC lacks any verification provisions and there are compliance concerns related to the CWC, particularly with regard to Syria. These challenges notwithstanding, the greatest challenge to establishing a WMDFZ in the Middle East is establishing a zone without nuclear weapons. As a first step in the right direction, the EU should play a constructive role by actively promoting the establishment of a nuclear-test-free zone in the region.

Is Turkey In the Middle East?

The political challenges to establishing a Middle East NWFZ become apparent when considering a seemingly simple and technical question: which countries should be included in the zone?

One approach is to follow the International Atomic Energy Agency (IAEA) definition of the Middle East region, which comprises the 21 state-members of the Arab League plus Iran and Israel.[2] This is also the definition used in the Draft Final Document of the 2015 Nuclear Non-Proliferation Treaty (NPT) Review Conference.[3] It differs, however, from more commonly understood definitions of the Middle East that include the following sixteen states: Bahrain, Cyprus, Egypt, Iran, Iraq, Israel, Jordan, Kuwait, Lebanon, Oman, Qatar, Saudi Arabia, Syria, Turkey, the United Arab Emirates, and Yemen.

The latter definition of the region is more logical than the one adopted by the United Nations and the IAEA. Indeed, it is hard to understand why, for example, the Comoros and Mauritania—but not Turkey—should be considered as part of the Middle East. Moreover, since Algeria, Libya, and Tunisia (as well as the Comoros and Mauritania) have ratified the Pelindaba Treaty, which came into force in 2009 and establishes a NWFZ in Africa, attempting to include them in a Middle East NWFZ would add complications but no value.

In any case, a NWFZ in the Middle East should obviously include Turkey, all the more so because of Turkey's commitment to the idea of such a zone. According to Carnegie Europe's Sinan Ülgen, "In recent years, Ankara has been advocating the implementation of a regional nuclear weapons–free zone, which officials see as part of an overall strategy to decrease tensions in the region."[4] Meanwhile, given Turkey's harboring of Saudi military aircraft at its Incirlik Air Base, as well as its involvement in Syria and elsewhere, it seems hypocritical for the United Nations to pretend that Turkey is not part of the Middle East when it comes to promoting a WMDFZ in that region.

However, including Turkey in a NWFZ in the Middle East would require the withdrawal of NATO's tactical nuclear weapons from Turkish territory. Under what conditions could one envisage such a withdrawal? Ülgen argues that it could take place only if "NATO was operating in consensus," meaning if Belgium, Germany, Italy, and the Netherlands, which are also non-nuclear-weapon states that host US tactical nuclear weapons, did the same.[5] That said, Ülgen also indicates that Turkey "quietly supports maintaining the weapons on its territory and expects other NATO countries to continue their tactical nuclear weapon stewardship as part of the Alliance's burden-sharing principle."6 Meanwhile, NATO members have discussed the possibility of removing nuclear weapons from Europe, but no consensus exists for unilateral withdrawal and any reciprocal agreement with Russia remains unlikely in the near future.

Peace or Security: Which Comes First?

Of course, the creation of a NWFZ in the Middle East would also mean requiring Israel to join the NPT and to give up its—not so ambiguous—nuclear deterrence policy. Yet, why do EU states ask Israel to do what they themselves are not prepared to do? Let's be honest: who is facing the greatest security threat? Is it Israel, or is it France, the UK, and four EU non-nuclear-weapon states that have nuclear weapons on their territories?[7]

In fact, advocating for non-NPT states to dismantle their nuclear arsenals before the five nuclear-weapon states do so, as they committed to do under the NPT more than 45 years ago, represents another illustration of the counterproductive policy of double standards that weakens the legitimacy of the NPT.

Within the Middle East, Egypt and other Arab states consider the possession of nuclear weapons by Israel to be a major obstacle to peace and security in the region, while Israel sees nuclear disarmament as a consequence of peace, not as a precondition of it.

This brings to mind what Salvador de Madariaga famously said in 1973:

> *The trouble with disarmament was (and still is) that the problem of war is tackled upside down and at the wrong end. . . . Nations don't distrust each other because they are armed; they are armed because they distrust each other. And therefore to want disarmament before a minimum of common agreement on fundamentals is as absurd as to want people to go undressed in winter. Let the weather be warm, and they will undress readily enough without committees to tell them so.*[8]

The current state of Israeli relations with Iran and Syria presents serious roadblocks to a NWFZ in the Middle East. The credibility of such a zone will rest on the establishment of a reciprocal inspection regime. Before one can hope to see Israeli inspectors in Iran and vice versa, Iran would have to recognize the existence of Israel and the two countries would have to establish normal diplomatic relations. Also, Syria and Israel would have to conclude a peace treaty and end the formal state of war existing between the two nations.

All these obstacles do not necessarily mean that the Middle East and the international community cannot achieve progress on a NWFZ, but they do indicate that there is an indispensable need to move from grand visions and rhetorical declarations to concrete confidence-building measures. Without an effort to first establish a regional political and security order, it is highly unlikely that the Middle East can effectively address arms control. International conferences alone are not sufficient to reach such a lofty goal.

The Nuclear Testing Lacuna

As of today, and contrary to Israel, neither India nor Pakistan has even signed the Comprehensive Nuclear-Test-Ban Treaty (CTBT).[9] Moreover, like Israel, the United States and China have signed but not ratified the CTBT, but nonetheless call for Israel to ratify it. This is just another example of a counterproductive "do what I say but not what I do" policy.

The conclusion of the US-Indian nuclear cooperation deal in 2005, and the subsequent consensus agreement of the then

46 members of the Nuclear Suppliers Group to waive the group's export criteria for India, has made matters worse. The privileged treatment thereby accorded to India, a non-NPT state, further diminishes the likelihood that two other non-NPT states, Pakistan and Israel, will join the NPT as non-nuclear-weapon states.

The nuclear normalization of India has come at the expense of the CTBT. On June 6, 1998, the UN Security Council unanimously adopted Resolution 1172 in which it urged "India and Pakistan, and all other States that have not yet done so, to become Parties to the Treaty on the Non-Proliferation of Nuclear Weapons and to the Comprehensive Nuclear Test Ban Treaty without delay and without conditions."[10]

Over a decade later, on September 24, 2009, the Security Council passed Resolution 1887 which "calls upon all States to refrain from conducting a nuclear test explosion and to sign and ratify the Comprehensive Nuclear Test Ban Treaty (CTBT), thereby bringing the treaty into force at an early date."[11]

UN Secretary General Ban Ki-moon rightfully declared in 2012 that "there is no good reason to avoid signing or ratifying this Treaty. Any country opposed to signing or ratifying it is simply failing to meet its responsibilities as a member of the international community."[12]

Let's Start with a Nuclear-Test-Free-Zone in the Middle East

It is unrealistic to expect Israel to join the NPT as a non-nuclear-weapon state anytime soon. But it is necessary to seek practical and balanced regional confidence-building measures. Since 2007, I have repeatedly advocated that the first such measure should be to promote a nuclear-test-free zone (NTFZ) in the Middle East under an agreement committing Egypt, Iran, Israel, Saudi Arabia, and Syria to ratify the CTBT in a coordinated way and within an agreed period of time.

The ratification of the CTBT by those five states would, de facto, establish a NTFZ in the Middle East since all other key countries in the region, including Turkey, have already ratified the CTBT.[13]

A nuclear-test-free zone in the Middle East would represent the first concrete step in building nuclear confidence in the region and would be a win-win measure for all concerned. It would not single out any state, and thus would not give any state an incentive to block progress. Moreover, it could occur without waiting for the recognition of Israel by Iran and many Arab states and the conclusion of a peace treaty between Israel and Syria.

If any state in the region considered only an all-or-nothing approach and rejected limited confidence-building steps, such as the one proposed here, that would provide clear evidence that such a state is not serious about establishing a WMDFZ in the Middle East and is in fact comfortable with the status quo.

Conclusion

The failure of the 2015 NPT Review Conference to produce a final document, although disappointing, was not a surprise. As Andrey Baklitskiy has observed, "The issue of the creation of a zone free of weapons of mass destruction (WMD) in the Middle East" was "the straw that broke the camel's back in 2015."[14]

Although there is no guarantee of success, it is obvious that the talks on this issue must continue. But taking the same approach as before does not bode well for the next NPT Review Conference in 2020. In the years until then, it is worth thinking outside the box and considering which practical steps and confidence-building measures can be implemented to both advance the prospects of a WMDFZ in the Middle East and bypass the obstacles that have prevented progress so far.

It is encouraging that the executive secretary of the Preparatory Commission for the Comprehensive Nuclear-Test-Ban Treaty Organization, Lassina Zerbo, said in January 2016 that having Iran and Israel ratify the CTBT together would "certainly" lead to ratification by Egypt, which would in turn help lead to a NTFZ in the Middle East.[15]

One EU member state—Cyprus—is part of the Middle East, and all 28 EU member states ratified the CTBT more than ten years ago. The EU is therefore in a good position to use its diplomatic skills to promote the establishment of a nuclear-test-free zone in the Middle East. This can—and should—be done immediately, regardless of the unstable political situation prevailing in the Middle East today.

Notes

1. Today there are no WMDFZs in the world, but there are five nuclear-weapon-free zones, including in Latin America and the Caribbean (Treaty of Tlatelolco), the South Pacific (Treaty of Rarotonga), and Africa (Treaty of Pelindaba).
2. International Atomic Energy Agency, "Application of IAEA Safeguards in the Middle East," Report by the Director General at the Board of Governors General Conference, September 2, 2011, https://www.iaea.org/About/Policy/GC/GC55/GC55Documents/English/gc55-23_en.pdf.
3. 2015 Review Conference of the Parties to the Treaty on the Non-Proliferation of Nuclear Weapons, "Draft Final Document: Volume I," May 21, 2015, http://www.reachingcriticalwill.org/images/documents/Disarmament-fora/npt/revcon2015/documents/DraftFinalDocument.pdf, 22.
4. Sinan Ülgen, "Turkey and the Bomb," Carnegie Endowment for International Peace, February 2012, http://carnegieendowment.org/files/turkey_bomb.pdf.
5. Ibid.
6. Ibid.
7. NATO, in its "Deterrence and Defence Posture Review," states, "Nuclear weapons are a core component of NATO's overall capabilities for deterrence and defence alongside conventional and missile defence forces." NATO, "Deterrence and Defence Posture Review," Press Release 063, May 20, 2012, http://www.nato.int/cps/en/natolive/official_texts_87597.htm.
8. Born in Spain, Professor Salvador de Madariaga (1886–1978) was an important writer, poet, historian, philosopher, and politician as well as a passionate defender of liberty and tolerance. He was the founder of the College of Europe. Salvador de Madariaga, *Morning Without Noon* (Westmead, UK: Saxon House, 1973), 48–49.
9. The Vienna Convention on the Law of the Treaties compels the parties that have signed a treaty not to act in a manner that would "defeat the object and purpose" of that instrument. Vienna Convention on the Law of Treaties, May 23, 1969, art. 18, 1155 UNTS 331, 336, available at: https://treaties.un.org/doc/Publication/UNTS/Volume%201155/volume-1155-I-18232-English.pdf.
10. United Nations Security Council, Resolution 1172, June 6, 1998, http://www.un.org/en/ga/search/view_doc.asp?symbol=S/RES/1172(1998).

11. United Nations Security Council, Resolution 1887, September 24, 2009, http://www.un.org/en/ga/search/view_doc.asp?symbol=S/RES/1887(2009).

12. Preparatory Commission for the Comprehensive Nuclear-Test-Ban Treaty Organization, "UN Secretary-General: Proud of 15 Years of Successful Fight Against Nuclear Testing, Urge Entry Into Force of the CTBT," press release, February 17, 2012, http://www.ctbto.org/press-centre/press-releases/2012/un-secretary-general-proud-of-15-years-of-successful-fight-against-nuclear-testing-urge-entry-into-force-of-the-ctbt/.

13. With the unimportant and hopefully temporary exceptions of Somalia and Yemen, all other members of the Arab League (including Iraq in 2013) have ratified the CTBT.

14. Andrey Baklitskiy, "The 2015 NPT Review Conference and the Future of the Nonproliferation Regime," *Arms Control Today* 45 (July/August 2015): https://www.armscontrol.org/ACT/2015_0708/Features/The-2015-NPT-Review-Conference-and-the-Future-of-The-Nonproliferation-Regime.

15. Edith M. Lederer, "UN Official: Iran, Israel Could Ratify Nuke Test Ban Treaty," Associated Press, January 29, 2016, http://bigstory.ap.org/article/cb8e7a27a6154133aad9f05c2603f62b/un-official-iran-israel-could-ratify-nuke-test-ban-treaty.

9

The Threat of Nuclear War Over Kashmir

Annie Waqar

Annie Waqar is a lecturer in the department of politics and international relations at the University of Westminster in the United Kingdom. Her research focuses on nuclear security in South Asia and the Middle East as well as defense, arms control, and international relations.

Since India became independent from British rule in 1947 and divided into two countries—Pakistan and India—control over the border region of Kashmir has been a major source of conflict. The tension is escalated by the fact that both countries are in possession of nuclear weapons, which they have threatened to use on one another. Waqar traces this conflict from the Indian Independence Act of 1947 to the present and explains the severity of the current nuclear threat in the region.

Of the numerous areas of global tension, arguably the most perilous is that between India and Pakistan. And recent events in Kashmir have made the situation even more dangerous. The reason is straightforward: India and Pakistan are in a long-running and incendiary dispute, they are both nuclear powers, and crossing a confrontational threshold could ignite a nuclear war between

"Nuclear War Between India and Pakistan? An Expert Assesses the Risks," by Annie Waqar, The Conversation, March 6, 2019, https://theconversation.com/nuclear-war-between-india-and-pakistan-an-expert-assesses-the-risk-112892.

them. Indeed, arms control investigators have long identified the subcontinent as one of the world's likeliest nuclear flashpoints.

India and Pakistan share a long and complicated history, and they have been in conflict over the disputed territory of Kashmir since 1947. The Himalayan region is one of the most militarised regions on Earth—former US president Bill Clinton has called Kashmir "the most dangerous place in the world."

Under the partition plan provided by the Indian Independence Act of 1947, Kashmir with its Muslim majority was free to accede to either India or Pakistan. But the local ruler, Hari Singh, decided against giving the population a choice, leaving the region in a geopolitical limbo and with a disputed border. A two-year war erupted between India and Pakistan in 1947 and another broke out in 1965. In 1999, the Kargil crisis, when the two countries again came to blows, may have been the closest the world has come to nuclear war since the end of World War II.

Diplomatic interventions have previously helped to defuse the military tensions, but an enduring peace has remained elusive. Both sides have dug in along the disputed border and military skirmishes are commonplace.

The Nuclear Question

It has long been argued in international security circles that having nuclear weapons deters countries from using them in warfare. Indeed, in the post-World War II era, no state has used them—despite there still being around 15,000 nuclear weapons in the world. But horizontal nuclear proliferation has made the world a dangerous place; the more countries that have them, the more likely they are to be used at some stage.

And while the presence of nuclear weapons may forestall a nuclear exchange, they don't discourage nuclear states from using conventional military power against one another. And, as conventional conflicts can quickly escalate, the possibility of a nuclear exchange remains a real, if remote, possibility.

So what are the chances of India and Pakistan (which both have between 130 and 150 warheads) engaging in a nuclear war?

The most recent escalation is just another example of the ongoing tensions between these nuclear neighbours. It was triggered by a Kashmiri militant suicide bombing of an Indian paramilitary convoy in mid February. In that attack, more than 40 people were killed, mostly Indian military personnel—and Jaish-e-Mohammed, an Islamist terrorist group situated in Pakistan, claimed responsibility for the attack.

Indian prime minister Narendra Modi, currently caught up in election fever, warned of a "crushing response," and launched air strikes on targets in the Pakistan-controlled Khyber Pakhtunkhwa province. It was not long before both sides were exchanging artillery fire across the line of control and the conflict quickly escalated.

Meanwhile, in a national televised speech, Pakistan's prime minister, Imran Khan, stated that any further escalation between the nations would be beyond the leaders' control, warning:

> *With the weapons you have and the weapons we have, can we afford miscalculation? Shouldn't we think that if this escalates, what will it lead to?*

The ball is now in India's court. Modi has the choice of escalating the conflict by deploying more jets into Pakistani territory, which could lead to a flurry of "tit-for-tat" retaliations. So what could be next?

Since 1974, when India stunned the world with its unexpected atomic trial of the "Smiling Buddha" weapon, South Asia has been viewed as a global nuclear problem. Nevertheless, to date, India, like China, has maintained a "No First Use" doctrine. This advocates that India will only use its nuclear weapons in response to a nuclear attack. The policy was proclaimed in 1999, a year after Pakistan effectively exploded five of its own nuclear weapons. But Pakistan has so far refused to issue any clear doctrine governing its own use of nuclear weapons.

The Stakes Are High

The combined arsenals of Pakistan and India are small compared to those of the US, Russia or China. Nevertheless, they are more powerful than those dropped on Japan in 1945 and could unleash staggering destruction if deployed on civilian targets. Indeed, even a constrained exchange of warheads between the two nations would, in a split second, be among the most calamitous ever, notwithstanding the risk of the radioactive aftermath and the long-term impact on the environment.

India's nuclear-powered ballistic missile submarine, INS Arihant, became operational in 2018, giving the country a "nuclear triad"—the ability to launch nuclear strikes by land, air and sea. Its other ground-based ballistic missile, the Agni III, has a range of approximately 3,000km.

While Pakistan has a slightly larger nuclear arsenal—estimated to be 140-150 warheads in 2017—it is less capable of delivering them to targets. Although Pakistan is developing new ballistic missiles, its current ballistic missile range is 2,000km and the country has no nuclear-armed submarines. Either way, it currently would take less than four minutes for a nuclear missile launched from Pakistan to reach India, and vice versa.

The worst case scenario is that, either through mishap or error, what began with a terrorist attack grows into a nuclear exchange aimed at one another's civilian populations. Technological advances might also exacerbate the already incendiary situation. India's arsenal now includes the BrahMos, a cruise missile developed jointly with Russia, which can be fired from land, sea or air and used as a counterforce weapon. Counterforce doctrine, in nuclear strategy, means the targeting of an opponent's military infrastructure with a nuclear strike.

Discontent in the Kashmir valley could also intensify and lead to further crises. No Indian government has thus far shown the political will to solve the Kashmir crisis, to demilitarise it, or to apply the diplomatic deftness needed to negotiate a solution with Pakistan. Nor has Modi been able to control and prevent hardline Hindus from forming vigilante squads in the region and threatening and killing those they think are defiling their religious convictions. And so, on a day-to-day basis, ordinary people continue to suffer.

In the past, during episodes of global tension, the US has taken the lead in crisis management. But it seems unlikely that Islamabad or New Delhi would now turn to the Trump administration for assistance in deescalating the conflict. Indeed, leaders from both countries must also consider the reaction of Asia's third nuclear power, China, which has always been the primary focus of India's nuclear program.

For now, India and Pakistan are showing some vital restraint. But they must also work towards a long-term fix. The last thing either government, or the world, needs is a mushroom cloud.

10

The Modern Nuclear Winter

David McCoy

David McCoy is a senior lecturer of public health at the Queen Mary University of London. He spent five years in clinical medicine before moving into the broader field of public health, which included seven years of post-apartheid transformation work in South Africa.

In 1945, America detonated two nuclear weapons over the cities of Hiroshima and Nagasaki with little ecological fallout outside of Japan. Modern technology has advanced drastically: McCoy mentions offhand that India and Pakistan share about one hundred Hiroshima-sized warheads, and that's considered small in the modern military landscape. Research seems to show that one hundred Hiroshima detonations—a relatively "small" nuclear conflict—may still prove to have devastating consequences for the ecology of the entire planet.

President Donald Trump's vow to hit North Korea with "fire and fury like the world has never seen" is an unveiled threat to unleash America's most potent weapons of mass destruction onto the Korean peninsula. According to many defence analysts, the risk of nuclear confrontation over Europe and the Indian subcontinent has also increased in recent years.

In a more hopeful turn of events, 122 countries voted in June to adopt the United Nations Treaty on the prohibition of nuclear weapons in New York. The "ban treaty" will make nuclear weapons illegal for ratifying countries, and many see it as an opportunity to kick start a renewed effort towards multilateral disarmament. Supporters of the treaty argue that even a limited, regional nuclear war would produce a catastrophic and global humanitarian crisis.

Equally, other analysts suggest that the reality is not as severe as is often depicted. In March this year, Matthias Eken, a researcher of attitudes towards nuclear weapons, wrote in The Conversation that their destructive power "has been vastly exaggerated" and that one should avoid overusing "doomsday scenarios and apocalyptic language."

Eken argued that nuclear weapons are not as powerful as often described, on the basis that a 9 megaton thermonuclear warhead dropped over the state of Arkansas would only destroy 0.2% of the state's surface area. He also observed that more than 2,000 nuclear detonations have been made on the planet without having ended human civilisation, and argued that if we want to mitigate the risk posed by nuclear weapons, we must not exaggerate those risks.

Eken's sanguine approach towards nuclear weapons stands in contrast to the more dramatic rhetoric of global humanitarian catastrophe and existential threats to humanity. So what is the basis for the latter?

Nuclear War Is Also a War on the Environment

The greatest concern derives from relatively new research which has modelled the indirect effects of nuclear detonations on the environment and climate. The most-studied scenario is a limited regional nuclear war between India and Pakistan, involving 100 Hiroshima-sized warheads (small by modern standards) detonated mostly over urban areas. Many analysts suggest that this is a plausible scenario in the event of an all-out war between the two states, whose combined arsenals amount to more than 220 nuclear warheads.

In this event, an estimated 20m people could die within a week from the direct effects of the explosions, fire, and local radiation.

That alone is catastrophic—more deaths than in the entire of World War I.

But nuclear explosions are also extremely likely to ignite fires over a large area, which coalesce and inject large volumes of soot and debris into the stratosphere. In the India-Pakistan scenario, up to 6.5m tonnes of soot could be thrown up into the upper atmosphere, blocking out the sun and causing a significant drop in average surface temperature and precipitation across the globe, with effects that could last for more than a decade.

This ecological disruption would, in turn, badly affect global food production. According to one study, maize production in the US (the world's largest producer) would decline by an average by 12% over ten years in our given scenario. In China, middle season rice would fall by 17% over a decade, maize by 16%, and winter wheat by 31%. With total world grain reserves amounting to less than 100 days of global consumption, such effects would place an estimated 2 billion people at risk of famine.

Although a nuclear conflict involving North Korea and the US would be smaller, given Pyongyang's limited arsenal, many people would still die and ecological damage would severely affect global public health for years. Additionally, any nuclear conflict between the US and North Korea is likely to increase the risk of nuclear confrontation involving other states and other regions of the world.

It Gets Worse

A large-scale nuclear war between the US and Russia would be far worse. Most Russian and US weapons are 10 to 50 times stronger than the bombs that destroyed Hiroshima. In a war involving the use of the two nations' strategic nuclear weapons (those intended to be used away from battlefield, aimed at infrastructure or cities), some 150m tonnes of soot could be lofted into the upper atmosphere. This would reduce global temperatures by 8°C—the "nuclear winter" scenario. Under these conditions, food production would stop and the vast majority of the human race is likely to starve.

Eken suggests that both the scenarios of a limited regional nuclear conflict and an all-out war between US and Russia are unlikely. He may be right. However, both scenarios are possible, even if we can't reliably quantify the risk. Continued adversarial rhetoric from both Donald Trump and Kim Jong-un about the use of nuclear weapons is not making this possibility any smaller.

What we can say, is that the doctrine of nuclear deterrence represents a high-risk gamble. Nuclear weapons do not keep us safe from acts of terrorism, nor can they be used to fight sea level rise, extreme weather, ocean acidification, biodiversity loss or antimicrobial resistance.

This is why so many medical and public health organisations have been campaigning to make nuclear weapons illegal. Regardless of how many need to be exploded to cause a catastrophe or produce an existential threat to humanity, and regardless of the risk of this happening, the adage that "prevention is the best cure" remains the case when it comes to these abhorrent and dangerous weapons.

11

How Nuclear Anxiety Affects Civilians

Susan T. Fiske

Susan Tufts Fiske is the Eugene Higgins Professor of Psychology and Public Affairs at Princeton University. She is a social psychologist whose research addresses how stereotyping, prejudice, and discrimination are encouraged or discouraged by social relationships.

The fear surrounding nuclear weapons presents a strange conundrum to the average person. It is a weapon capable of large-scale destruction, and the use of it is largely out of the hands of civilians and at the whim of their leaders. In this excerpted viewpoint from Fiske, the focus moves away from the international scene to glimpse at the effect of nuclear anxiety on a personal, psychological level. Fiske concludes that a layman's inaction in the face of nuclear destruction is professionally reasonable—whether that is unnerving or comforting is open for interpretation.

I would like to begin with a story. I have a friend who has cancer, and she has reason to believe that she has a one-third chance of dying from it. She understands this diagnosis, but her possible death remains somewhat hypothetical to her. She imagines it mostly in the abstract, and she talks about missing the city and her occasional trips into the country. She does not talk so much about missing the people in her life. She believes she cannot do anything to change her odds. She does not worry about it very often; it

"Adult Beliefs, Feelings, and Actions Regarding Nuclear War: Evidence from Surveys and Experiments," by Susan T. Fiske PhD, *The Medical Implications of Nuclear War,* Fredric Solomon, ed. National Academies Press. Reprinted by permission.

mostly is not salient to her. If asked about it, she reports fear and worry, and certainly she prefers effective treatment to nothing. But she does not change her life with regard to her cancer. She does not seek support. She does not join organizations. She does not discuss her situation publicly. She goes on about her normal life. Some people say she is marvelous, remarkable, life-affirming, brave, and adaptable. Other people say she is suppressing her fear, denying reality, and desensitized to her own death.

My friend is the average American citizen. Her cancer is the possibility of a nuclear war. This portrait of her reactions resembles the portrait I will draw of the ordinary person's reactions to the possibility of nuclear war. I have described it this way initially because it is becoming difficult to have a fresh perspective on this issue. I will come back to this point at the end, but it may be useful to keep the story in mind while reading this paper.

[…]

With respect to most issues, people's beliefs, feelings, and actions are fairly consistent; such consistency enables psychological equilibrium. In the context of nuclear war, however, there are major discrepancies between the ordinary person's beliefs, on the one hand, and the ordinary person's feelings and actions, on the other hand. Although this observation is not entirely new, there has been little effort to review the hard data concerning the modal person's beliefs, feelings, and actions.[1] The sources of data include more than 50 studies from social and behavioral science: mainly surveys of adults, with preference given to national findings, where available, over local findings; some questionnaire studies of college students; and a few experimental studies with college students. The data span a period from 1945 to the present, and they lend some new insights into the discrepancies among people's beliefs, feelings, and actions.

Modal Beliefs About Nuclear War

People think of nuclear war as somewhat unlikely, imagining mainly complete material destruction, in the abstract, with themselves definitely not surviving.

Psychologists have long attempted to document people's beliefs about nuclear war, primarily using survey interviews and questionnaires, but also drawing on the in-depth relationship of the clinical setting. Immediately following the bombings of Hiroshima and Nagasaki, the first surveys began to examine people's attitudes toward the bomb and its use. Attitude surveys ebbed and flowed over the next four decades, peaking after the Russians' first atomic test, the creation of the hydrogen bomb, the Bay of Pigs and Cuban Missile Crisis, the Nuclear Test Ban Treaty, the Strategic Arms Limitation Treaty (SALT) initiatives, and during the present unprecedented level of worldwide concern over nuclear weapons. The number of surveys reflects variations in levels of public interest, as indicated by citation frequencies in the *Reader's Guide to Periodical Literature*.

Complementing the survey efforts, some clinical psychologists and psychiatrists have lately begun to note the intrusion of concerns about nuclear war within the therapy hour.

This review of the survey data will suggest that ordinary people's nuclear war beliefs have changed remarkably little over the four eventful decades since the bombings of Hiroshima and Nagasaki. Despite massive technological change in the power of the weapons and in their delivery time, despite their considerable proliferation, and despite dramatic fluctuations in the geopolitical situation, we will see that the adult American's response has endured with remarkable consistency. Moreover, people's responses differ surprisingly little across age, gender, race, education, income, and political ideology. Apparently this is one thing on which ordinary citizens agree, and have agreed, for decades.

Most important, people view nuclear war as not very probable, a hypothetical event. The average person views nuclear war as fairly unlikely within the next 10 years.[2] A local survey in Pittsburgh found that, on average, people estimated a one-third chance of a nuclear war within their lifetimes, and a local sample in Chicago put the estimate at one-half. Three decades ago, people were asked about the likelihood of another world war, which they overwhelmingly believed would be nuclear; they viewed such a war as somewhat more likely than people do now, but the average person still estimated the chances as 50/50. People are considerably more pessimistic about the possibility of nuclear war if a conventional war should erupt. Since 1946, between 63 and 79 percent of Americans have believed that any subsequent major war would necessarily be nuclear. Overall, however, the indications are that people now view nuclear war as unlikely, on balance.

If the hypothetical were to occur, people expect it would be horrific. As early as 1954 and as recently as 1982, survey respondents described similar images of the event and its aftermath.[3] Two features of these descriptions are notable. First, material destruction is described more than human destruction, and second, abstract content outweighs concrete content. This primary emphasis on the material and abstract, rather than on concrete human devastation, is in marked contrast to the descriptions of Hiroshima survivors, who focus almost entirely on the human misery.

[...]

Modal Feelings About Nuclear War

People worry seldom, but they overwhelmingly favor a mutual nuclear freeze.

The beliefs people commonly report about a nuclear holocaust are bleak, which implies that people should also report some concomitant emotional reactions. When asked directly what emotions come to mind regarding a nuclear war, the typical person does report fear, terror, and worry or fear and sadness. On the whole, however, most people do not frequently think about nuclear war. The typical adult apparently worries seldom or relatively little about the possibility. And such emotional responses do not vary dramatically as a function of social class or overall political ideology.

[...]

More generally, people's level of nuclear anxiety is related to nonconforming attitudes, felt vulnerability, drug use, low self-esteem, and perceived lack of social support. Similarly, nuclear anxiety is related to death anxiety. Of course, the direction of causality is not clear. People who experience nuclear anxiety may therefore be more vulnerable socially and emotionally, but the reverse is equally possible: people who are vulnerable for other reasons may then focus disproportionately on the nuclear threat. These are promising lines of inquiry, but the data on these matters are only beginning to come in.

Clinical interviews—with less representative samples but with more depth—indicate deep-seated worry, fear, and anxiety on the part of some individuals. These individuals are not typical of the larger population, however, so unfortunately, we do not know whether the interviews uncovered something about those particular people or a deeper truth about all of us.

The essential research requires both in-depth interviews and representative samples; it apparently remains to be done. Nevertheless, the best current evidence indicates that, although people report concern when asked, for most people, most of the time, the issue is not emotionally central.

People's feelings about nuclear war emerge more dramatically, however, in their policy preferences. The typical person clearly supports a mutual freeze on nuclear arms, although not a unilateral freeze. Support for a mutual freeze is remarkably consensual (77 percent agree); it is unusually broad based, showing few differences across gender, age, income, and education; and it has held firm over the decades since 1945. The typical person believes that the use of atomic weapons in Japan was necessary and proper but does not accept their use any longer.

[...]

Modal Actions Regarding Nuclear War

Most people do nothing.

The typical person does not act in any way that goes beyond voicing support for the policy of a nuclear freeze. Age, gender, and social class are not reliable predictors of activism, although political ideology may be. Most people simply do not write antinuclear letters to the editor or to their elected representatives, they do not join or financially support the relevant organizations, and they do not sign petitions. From one perspective, given people's nuclear war beliefs, including the low likelihood of personal survival and their at least minimal worry, they might be expected to be more active. What is especially surprising, to some observers, is that people are inactive in a matter of such literally earth-shattering consequence. From another perspective, however, the inaction of ordinary citizens is not at all surprising, for most people most of the time pay scant attention to politics and almost never engage in political activity beyond voting, if that. Moreover, with regard to this particular issue, there is no evidence that people expect their actions to have consequences; that is, they have a low sense of political efficacy.

[...]

Conclusion

Decades ago psychologists anticipated people's fears about the bomb; they initially worked to assuage these fears, to promote public trust in the atomic experts, and to examine civil defense from a psychological perspective. But these efforts soon tapered off as it became clear that, surprisingly, the ordinary person was apparently less concerned than the researchers expected. Despite high levels of reported awareness about the issues, people report relatively little fear or worry, at least in survey interviews, and most people take no action to prevent nuclear war. Many observers have wondered publicly about the ordinary citizen's apparent indifference when confronted with the potential annihilation of humankind. These contrasts have prompted the enduring puzzle variously called fear suppression, psychic numbing, denial, and apathy, which are attributed to people's feelings of impotence, helplessness, inefficacy, and the like. The discrepancy between people's nuclear understanding and their elusive emotional and behavioral concern continues to be a puzzle.

Most participants in the symposium on which this proceedings volume is based and most readers of this book probably agree that nuclear war is an important issue, as shown by their involvement. But our personal and professional involvement in this issue has a risk. It creates a danger of what social psychologists call a false consensus bias; that is, it is too easy to believe that the average citizen shams a sense of urgency, shams a sense that something must be done. The false consensus biases us to believe that others share our attitudes. Becoming aware of the false consensus bias means realizing that, for the average citizen, the issue is not all that salient. We must not overestimate the degree of disturbance in the average person. Although they are clearly aware and deeply concerned, nuclear war, for the most part, is not on their minds. The average person is also low on political efficacy, which is probably in contrast to the majority of readers and symposium participants. But most people's inaction is consistent with their understanding of political reality. We must not judge people by our own values.

Remaining relatively unworried and inactive, despite the horrific possibility of nuclear war, is not irrational if people are correct in judging that their activism would have no consequences. The ordinary person does not possess the antinuclear activist's sense of political efficacy, does not believe that nuclear war is preventable by citizen actions. And, according to some analysts, people are right about this: the activity of one ordinary person hardly makes a difference. Some observers argue that even collective public opinion rarely influences foreign policy; they rank public opinion far behind perceived geopolitical realities in influencing government leaders' decisions in this realm. Some experts even argue that the public is not competent to judge in these matters anyway. If one accepts all these premises, then ordinary people's relative lack of worry and complete inaction, despite their horrific beliefs and clear expectation that they would die in a nuclear war, are not irrational. Viewed this way, one can come to the defense of the ordinary person, and there is no massive problem revealed by the discrepancy in beliefs, feelings, and action about nuclear war.

[...]

Notes

1. This is partly because much of the relevant hard data are only now being generated. Hence, this article, of necessity, cites several unpublished papers and convention presentations.
2. Roughly a quarter of the population view it as very unlikely, a quarter as fairly unlikely, and a quarter as fairly likely; the remainder say it is very likely or express no opinion (The Gallup Poll, 1983).
3. An image, for these purposes, is a conception, an impression, or an understanding; it is a mental picture, but not necessarily visual. Readers familiar with the concept of a cognitive *schema* may wish to substitute that term for *image*. Image is used here to minimize jargon and because of its connotations of something gleaned through public channels such as the media. See Fiske et al. (1983) for a fuller discussion of these issues.

12

The Question of Civil Nuclear Defense

Steve Weintz

Steve Weintz is a writer, filmmaker, artist, animator, former firefighter, archaeologist, and stuntman.

According to this viewpoint, civil nuclear defense should be given as much consideration by the government as nuclear offense. But what does nuclear defense truly look like, and what is the scope of it? Weintz revisits the idea of nuclear bunkers and the various proposals that surfaced during the Eisenhower administration to reassess their viability. Weintz ends with a startling note that, considering the American policy of deterrence, perhaps defense is the best offense.

The proposed project was stupendous—about half the US GDP in 1957—but the goal was the preservation of 86 percent of the American people from a global thermonuclear war.

The special terror in nuclear deterrence reveals itself during natural rather than human-made disasters. Despite early warnings, extensive transport networks, government preparations and lots of money, thousands still suffer in the aftermath of great storms and fires. Nuclear-tipped ICBMs arrive with the surprise and speed of earthquakes, leaving whole populations sitting like ducks before the fury.

The devastation wrought by the great bombing raids of World War II, culminating in the atomic strikes on Hiroshima and

"America's Nuclear War Survival Plan if Russia Attacked: Massive Bunkers Under Every US City," by Steve Weintz, Center for the National Interest, November 10, 2018. Reprinted by permission.

Nagasaki, reinforced a cave-dwelling mindset that arose from the trenches of World War I and the rise of air power in the interwar years of the twentieth century. Early in the Atomic Age it seemed that the bunker building undertaken during the war could be extended in magnitude. As the bombs got bigger, however, the plans for shelter got wilder.

Two factors complicated civil defense from nuclear attack: hazard and numbers. Nuclear weapon effects are so enormous that extreme protective measures are necessary, yet the costs of thus protecting large populations quickly become astronomical. Those costs are not just in the vast constructions required, but also the major social rearrangements demanded of long-term communal shelter life.

Still, answers were found to President Dwight Eisenhower's 1956 question to the Gaither Committee on civil defense: "If you make the assumption that there is going to be a nuclear war, what should I do?"

One answer came from the wizards of the coast—the RAND Corporation think tank in Santa Monica, California. A man working with Herman Kahn, a large, big-idea thinker about nuclear war, suggested that if escape horizontally from the cities weren't possible, then the cities should escape vertically—deep underground.

The superb blog Atomic Skies lays out the plan in detail, and what a plan it was. Robert Panero, the likely source of the concept, oversaw a Ford Foundation-funded study in 1957–58 that looked into digging vast bunker complexes under every major American city. Shelters for hundreds of thousands of people would be excavated eight hundred feet below the cities, deep enough to avoid even multi-megaton city-busting H-bombs. Shelter entrances as large as shopping-mall gates and as ubiquitous as subway stairs would connect to giant rampways able to move thousands to shelter within minutes.

Safe within their cavern-towns, the citizens would submit to wartime regimentation, sleeping in huge dormitories and eating in vast cafeterias under the supervision of cadres, exercising and bathing in groups. Americans then and now seem unlikely candidates for such stiff social structure.

The proposed project was stupendous—about half the US GDP in 1957—but the goal was the preservation of 86 percent of the American people from a global thermonuclear war. Kahn & Panero's proposal was vast, comprehensive and detailed. It also nearly killed civil defense.

Spurgeon Keeney, a member of the Gaither Committee, wrote of the social consequences of shelter regimentation:

> *We became increasingly convinced that the distortion of society [by this] would be such [that] no one would tolerate it. . . There was no longer any question but that in a nuclear war you would lose the whole society, even though you could save lives with fallout shelters. The whole experience was extremely disturbing to me and many of the other participants. Was this really a way to solve the problem? The proposed solution seemed to lead to a garrison state.*

In 1959, something more congenial to the American way of life was envisioned by the students at the Cornell College of Architecture. In Professor Frederick Edmondson's classes they worked out a detailed plan for a post–apocalyptic company town.

The nine thousand inhabitants of the proposed Schoharie Valley Township in upstate New York could enter their communal bomb shelters via the elementary schools and downtown buildings, survive a twenty-megaton strike ten miles away, and keep the factory running and the kids in school until the fallout died down.

The shelters and connecting tunnels would spend most of their days as community resources—meeting halls, shopping malls and additional transit corridors. But like many college projects, the potentially-workable Schoharie Valley Township project vanished despite its impressive list of corporate and government backers.

By framing the true scale of the problem, the RAND men may have frightened workable solutions away. President Eisenhower's response to the Gaither Committee's findings was grim as only a soldier's can be: "You can't have this kind of war. There just aren't enough bulldozers to scrape the bodies off the streets."

The history of civil defense in America is one of long neglect and avoidance since the Cuban Missile Crisis. "[P]eople just didn't want to think about it . . . [I]f bomb shelters reduced casualties from, say, 100 million to 50 million, that still means tens of millions of dead," says Mark, the author of Atomic Skies. Other than rusting yellow-and-black "Fallout Shelter" signs on public buildings, almost nothing remains of American civil defense efforts.

And it need not have been, nor need it be. Switzerland, for example began a most thorough program of shelter construction decades ago, by legally requiring all new construction to incorporate shelters. By the 1980s over 80 percent of the Swiss population had immediate access to hardened protection. As Herman Kahn argued, nuclear deterrence only works if your opponent believes you'll risk Los Angeles for Moscow or Beijing. Serious civil defense makes such a threat credible; vacuous civilities about defense endanger everyone.

13

Nuclear War Is Less Likely Than It Might Seem

John Mueller

John Mueller is an adjunct professor of political science at the Mershon Center for International Security Studies of the University of Ohio. He has written various books, including The Remnants of War*—which won the Joseph Lepgold Prize for international relations in 2004—and* Overblown: How Politicians and the Terrorism Industry Inflate National Security Threats.

Making a case to keep calm and work past our nuclear fears is pretty difficult in the current geopolitical climate—even more so than it was when this viewpoint was originally published in 2010. That said, Mueller presents an argument in this excerpted viewpoint that may still help quell atomic anxiety in the current age. Though Mueller extensively addresses the idea of atomic terrorism—which has seemingly become less of a concern over the past decade—his overall message that nuclear weapons are fundamentally too expensive and too valuable as a deterrent to actually detonate continues to resonate and offer reassurance.

The fearsome destructive power of nuclear weapons provokes understandable dread, but in crafting public policy we must move beyond this initial reaction to soberly assess the risks and consider appropriate actions. Out of awe over and anxiety about nuclear weapons, the world's super-powers accumulated enormous

Mueller, John. "Calming Our Nuclear Jitters." *Issues in Science and Technology* 26, no. 2 (Winter 2010).

arsenals of them for nearly 50 years. But then, in the wake of the Cold War, fears that the bombs would be used vanished almost entirely. At the same time, concerns that terrorists and rogue nations could acquire nuclear weapons have sparked a new surge of fear and speculation.

In the past, excessive fear about nuclear weapons led to many policies that turned out to be wasteful and unnecessary. We should take the time to assess these new risks to avoid an overreaction that will take resources and attention away from other problems. Indeed, a more thoughtful analysis will reveal that the new perceived danger is far less likely than it might at first appear.

Albert Einstein memorably proclaimed that nuclear weapons "have changed everything except our way of thinking." But the weapons actually seem to have changed little except our way of thinking, as well as our ways of declaiming, gesticulating, deploying military forces, and spending lots of money.

To begin with, the bomb's impact on substantive historical developments has turned out to be minimal. Nuclear weapons are, of course, routinely given credit for preventing or deterring a major war during the Cold War era. However, it is increasingly clear that the Soviet Union never had the slightest interest in engaging in any kind of conflict that would remotely resemble World War II, whether nuclear or not. Its agenda emphasized revolution, class rebellion, and civil war, conflict areas in which nuclear weapons are irrelevant. Thus, there was no threat of direct military aggression to deter. Moreover, the possessors of nuclear weapons have never been able to find much military reason to use them, even in principle, in actual armed conflicts.

Although they may have failed to alter substantive history, nuclear weapons have inspired legions of strategists to spend whole careers agonizing over what one analyst has called "nuclear metaphysics," arguing, for example, over how many MIRVs (multiple independently targetable reentry vehicles) could dance on the head of an ICBM (intercontinental ballistic missile). The result was a colossal expenditure of funds.

Most important for current policy is the fact that contrary to decades of hand-wringing about the inherent appeal of nuclear weapons, most countries have actually found them to be a substantial and even ridiculous misdirection of funds, effort, and scientific talent. This is a major if much-underappreciated reason why nuclear proliferation has been so much slower than predicted over the decades.

In addition, the proliferation that has taken place has been substantially inconsequential. When the quintessential rogue state, Communist China, obtained nuclear weapons in 1964, Central Intelligence Agency Director John McCone sternly proclaimed that nuclear war was "almost inevitable." But far from engaging in the nuclear blackmail expected at the time by almost everyone, China built its weapons quietly and has never made a real nuclear threat.

[...]

Policy Alternatives

The purpose here has not been to argue that policies designed to inconvenience the atomic terrorist are necessarily unneeded or unwise. Rather, in contrast with the many who insist that atomic terrorism under current conditions is rather likely—indeed, exceedingly likely—to come about, I have contended that it is hugely unlikely. However, it is important to consider not only the likelihood that an event will take place, but also its consequences. Therefore, one must be concerned about catastrophic events even if their probability is small, and efforts to reduce that likelihood even further may well be justified.

At some point, however, probabilities become so low that, even for catastrophic events, it may make sense to ignore them or at least put them on the back burner; in short, the risk becomes acceptable. For example, the British could at any time attack the United States with their submarine-launched missiles and kill millions of Americans, far more than even the most monumentally gifted and lucky terrorist group. Yet the risk that this potential calamity might take place evokes little concern; essentially it is an acceptable risk. Meanwhile, Russia, with whom the United States has a rather strained relationship, could at any time do vastly more damage with its nuclear weapons, a fully imaginable calamity that is substantially ignored.

In constructing what he calls "a case for fear," Cass Sunstein, a scholar and current Obama administration official, has pointed out that if there is a yearly probability of 1 in 100,000 that terrorists could launch a nuclear or massive biological attack, the risk would cumulate to 1 in 10,000 over 10 years and to 1 in 5,000 over 20. These odds, he suggests, are "not the most comforting." Comfort, of course, lies in the viscera of those to be comforted, and, as he suggests, many would probably have difficulty settling down with odds like that. But there must be some point at which the concerns even of these people would ease. Just perhaps it is at one of the levels suggested above: one in a million or one in three billion per attempt.

As for that other central policy concern, nuclear proliferation, it seems to me that policymakers should maintain their composure. The pathetic North Korean regime mostly seems to be engaged in a process of extracting aid and recognition from outside. A viable policy toward it might be to reduce the threat level and to wait while continuing to be extorted, rather than to carry out policies that increase the already intense misery of the North Korean people.

If the Iranians do break their pledge not to develop nuclear weapons (a conversion perhaps stimulated by an airstrike on its facilities), they will probably "use" any nuclear capacity in the same way all other nuclear states have: for prestige (or ego-stoking) and deterrence. Indeed, suggests strategist and Nobel laureate Thomas Schelling, deterrence is about the only value the weapons might have for Iran. Nuclear weapons, he points out, "would be too precious to give away or to sell" and "too precious to waste killing people" when they could make other countries "hesitant to consider military action."

It seems overwhelmingly probable that, if a nuclear Iran brandishes its weapons to intimidate others or to get its way, it will find that those threatened, rather than capitulating to its blandishments or rushing off to build a compensating arsenal of their own, will ally with others, including conceivably Israel, to stand up to the intimidation. The popular notion that nuclear weapons furnish a country with the capacity to dominate its region has little or no historical support.

The application of diplomacy and bribery in an effort to dissuade these countries from pursuing nuclear weapons programs may be useful; in fact, if successful, we would be doing them a favor. But although it may be heresy to say so, the world can live with a nuclear Iran or North Korea, as it has lived now for 45 years with a nuclear China, a country once viewed as the ultimate rogue.

Should push eventually come to shove in these areas, the problem will be to establish orderly deterrent and containment strategies and to avoid the temptation to lash out mindlessly at fancied threats. Although there is nothing wrong with making nonproliferation a high priority, it should be topped with a somewhat higher one: avoiding policies that can lead to the deaths of tens or hundreds of thousands of people under the obsessive sway of worst-case scenario fantasies.

In the end, it appears to me that, whatever their impact on activist rhetoric, strategic theorizing, defense budgets, and political posturing, nuclear weapons have had at best a quite limited effect on history, have been a substantial waste of money and effort, do not seem to have been terribly appealing to most states that do not have them, are out of reach for terrorists, and are unlikely to materially shape much of our future.

14

What Is Nuclear Non-Proliferation?

Ian Johnstone

Ian Johnstone is the interim dean and a professor of international law at the Fletcher School of Law and Diplomacy of Tufts University. He previously served in the United Nations' Executive Office of the Secretary-General.

Though it has been many years since the international community created the Nuclear Non-Proliferation Treaty (NPT) in 1968, Johnstone argues that the treaty continues to be relevant in the current age and is a cause for optimism. However, he notes that the possibility of rapid nuclear proliferation by countries around the world should still cause concern, pointing out some of the signs of instability. However, despite the existence of legitimate concerns surrounding proliferation, Johnstone remains optimistic that non-proliferation will win out.

Iran recently exceeded the limits on uranium enrichment set out in its nuclear deal with the US and five other countries. Iran's move was in response to the US's renunciation of the same deal last May.

Possession of the uranium doesn't put Iran much closer to developing a nuclear weapon, but it does raise troubling questions about the future of nuclear nonproliferation.

Iran's leadership has also twice threatened to withdraw from a separate pact that limits the spread of nuclear weapons, the Nuclear Non-Proliferation Treaty. If Iran does withdraw from the treaty, it will be just the second country to do so, after North Korea in 2003, whose withdrawal has never been formally accepted.

But what is the Nuclear Non-Proliferation Treaty? And how serious is Iran's threat of withdrawal?

190 Countries Have Signed

In 1961, 16 years after the US dropped two atomic bombs on Japan, a U.N. resolution called for a treaty to stop the spread of nuclear weapons. The fear was that without such a treaty, as many as 25 countries could acquire nuclear weapons.

The U.N. resolution prompted the US and the Soviet Union to prepare drafts that became the basis for negotiations.

The treaty was opened for signing in 1968 and came into force in 1970 when 46 states had ratified it, including the US, UK and USSR. Today, the Nuclear Non-Proliferation Treaty has 190 parties —more than any other arms limitation treaty.

The treaty prohibits states that don't have nuclear weapons from acquiring them. It also prohibits the five nuclear state parties from helping others to acquire them, while pledging to work toward nuclear disarmament themselves. Compliance with the treaty is verified by the International Atomic Energy Agency and enforced by the U.N. Security Council.

Five states that possess nuclear weapons have signed the treaty: the US, UK, France, Russia and China.

Four additional nuclear states are not parties to the treaty: India, Pakistan, Israel and—most recently—North Korea.

With the 50th anniversary of the treaty around the corner, the Iran and North Korea crises are once again raising the specter of rapid proliferation—casting into doubt the value of the Nuclear Non-Proliferation Treaty. As a law professor who studies multilateral approaches to peace and security, I can identify some worrying signs.

For example, last year Saudi Crown Prince Mohamed Bin Salman said "if Iran develops a nuclear bomb, we will follow suit." He said this even though Saudi Arabia signed the Nuclear Non-Proliferation Treaty in 1988.

If Saudi Arabia joins Iran and Israel as a member of the nuclear club in the Middle East, how will Egypt, Turkey and others in the region respond?

If talks with North Korea on denuclearizing the Korean peninsula go nowhere and it is allowed to keep its current stockpile of 10-20 weapons for the indefinite future, how will Japan and South Korea react?

What's worse: The Nuclear Non-Proliferation Treaty isn't the only nuclear treaty on shaky ground.

President Trump announced in February 2019 that the US would withdraw from the Intermediate Nuclear Forces Treaty unless Russia eliminates one category of nuclear missiles that the US claims exceed the treaty limit.

And the 2010 Strategic Arms Reduction Treaty is due to expire in 2020. National Security Adviser John Bolton has called its extension "unlikely."

The end of these two important treaties could undermine the Nuclear Non-Proliferation Treaty by reinforcing a perception among nonnuclear parties that the nuclear states are not fulfilling their obligation "to pursue negotiations in good faith … on nuclear disarmament."

Reasons for Optimism

While worry about future proliferation is certainly warranted, I'd still argue that the Nuclear Non-Proliferation Treaty is alive and well.

Arguments to the contrary are based on two misconceptions.

The first is that the viability of the treaty depends primarily on fulfillment of the "grand bargain" embodied in it: that nonnuclear states agree not to acquire nuclear weapons in exchange for the nuclear states agreeing to eventually disarm and to assist other parties to develop peaceful nuclear energy. But the policies of nuclear states are not what motivates the nuclear decisions of other Nuclear Non-Proliferation Treaty parties. Most are motivated by regional security threats or by a conventional weapons attack by a perceived enemy.

For North Korea, going nuclear may look like the answer to perceived threats from the US and South Korea. For many, however, strengthening the global norm against proliferation through nuclear abstinence is a more promising approach.

The second misconception is that the treaty is suffering from a "crisis of noncompliance." The argument here is that the treaty didn't stop Iraq, Libya or North Korea from starting programs or prevent Iran from building substantial nuclear capacity, so it must be useless.

Yet perfect compliance is too demanding a measure of success of any law. Our society still values laws against thievery and tax evasion even though people break them every day.

Moreover, the Nuclear Non-Proliferation Treaty's record of compliance even in Iraq, Libya and North Korea is far from an unmitigated failure. The U.N. Security Council imposed a comprehensive disarmament regime on Iraq. Libya voluntarily gave up its program. North Korea's withdrawal from the Nuclear Non-Proliferation Treaty led to sanctions. Iran has never come within a year of being able to build a bomb.

How much of this is due to the Nuclear Non-Proliferation Treaty is open to debate, but pointing to a few cases of noncompliance does not prove its irrelevance.

As I argue in my book about the power of deliberation, a better way of gauging the value of the Nuclear Non-Proliferation Treaty is to ask whether it tips the scales against proliferation. Parties to the treaty will pay a price if caught cheating. They may decide the price is worth paying, but it is not cost-free. Compliance becomes the default position.

The Nuclear Non-Proliferation Treaty may have been bent by recent hits, but it is not broken.

15

How Domestic Policies Can Lead to a World Without Nuclear Weapons

The World Future Council

The World Future Council is a Germany-based independent organization that researches, identifies, and spreads policy solutions that contribute to sustainable development. It works with governments, businesses, and organizations around the world.

Nuclear weapon-free zones (NWFZ) are regions around the world that are committed to not partaking in the manufacture, acquisition, or possession of nuclear weapons. According to the World Future Council, these zones have played an important role in facilitating global nuclear disarmament, and as such focusing more on national and regional policies going forward would be the best way to encourage further disarmament. The viewpoint considers examples of successful legislation around the world and encourages countries to divest from producers of nuclear weapons.

The establishment of Nuclear Weapon-Free Zones (NWFZ) in the past has made invaluable contributions to global nuclear disarmament. The further spread of such zones as well as adoption of domestic nuclear prohibition and divestment policies can pave the way for multilateral solutions. The World Future Council has developed proposals on how to further foster nuclear disarmament through national and regional policies.

"Achieving a World Without Nuclear Weapons: The Contribution of Domestic and Regional Policies," The World Future Council, May 28, 2016. Reprinted by permission.

Nuclear weapons are a global threat which requires a global solution. However, domestic and regional policies can make a vital contribution to advancing universal nuclear disarmament. While the treaties establishing the existing regional Nuclear Weapon-Free Zones are well known and generally regarded as critical contributions to global nuclear disarmament (together covering 114 states), the instances of national nuclear prohibition legislation and nuclear divestment policies have not received the same amount of attention or, indeed, credit. This is unfortunate as these policies have advanced nuclear disarmament, can inspire other countries to follow suit and contain lessons for the global disarmament endeavour.

Between 2 May and 13 May 2016 the Open-Ended Working Group (OEWG) met for a second round in Geneva to discuss proposals to take forward multilateral nuclear disarmament negotiations for the achievement and maintenance of a world without nuclear weapons. The OEWG was established on the basis of a UN General Assembly resolution. Among the participants were numerous countries (though notably absent were all the nuclear-armed states), advocacy groups, research institutes, academic institutes and think tanks, including the World Future Council.

From Domestic to International—Stories of Successful Legislation

Some countries, such as New Zealand, the Philippines, Austria and Mongolia have banned nuclear weapons through national legislation. These policies have contributed to strengthening the nuclear prohibition norm and addressed specific security challenges.

Some of the laws contain innovative elements such as individual responsibility and extraterritorial application in the case of the New Zealand law, which prohibits New Zealand's citizens and residents to manufacture, to acquire, to possess or to control nuclear weapons as well as to aid and to abet any other person to do so anywhere in the world. These aspects of the policy could be useful to multilateral efforts to criminalise nuclear weapons employment such as through the Rome Statute for the International Criminal Court.

In the case of Mongolia, the country's subsequent work to have its nuclear weapon-free status recognised and respected through acquiring assurances by the nuclear-armed states they won't target Mongolia with nuclear weapons, means its policy is seen to have acquired the status of "Single State NWFZ."

All policies contain elements and lessons that could be considered in the pursuit of similar policies elsewhere. The triggering effect of single countries building a regime of domestic regional nuclear disarmament law should not be underestimated.

For example, Belgium adopted national legislation banning landmines and cluster munitions as well as any investment in such weapons, before the international processes that would ultimately culminate in the 1997 Mine Ban Treaty and the 2008 Convention on Cluster Munitions had started. This demonstrates how domestic legislative initiatives can inspire, strengthen and shape the international processes that culminate in international disarmament treaties.

Banning Investment in Nuclear Weapons

Divestment of landmines and cluster munitions producers has successfully been adopted in a number of countries. Divestment from corporations involved in the production of key components of nuclear weapons has not been pursued with the same vigour, though the Norwegian and New Zealand Government Pension Funds have implemented such schemes. More recently, the Swiss War Materials Act was revised to prohibit, *inter alia*, the financing of nuclear weapon producers. The effect of such divestment policies should not be underestimated. They contribute to stigmatising nuclear weapons and address the financial streams tied up in their production.

An interesting aspect of both nuclear prohibition and divestment policies is that they can lead to the democratisation of the nuclear disarmament debate, as they often originate from public movements and require legislators to become active on the issue. Furthermore, such policies can institutionalize nuclear disarmament expertise and commitment through the creation of organs committed to promoting policy objectives as well as become educational tools, both domestically and abroad. Perhaps most importantly, they offer a way for non-nuclear weapon states to take the initiative out of the hands of the nuclear-armed states, brandish their nuclear disarmament credentials, codify nuclear disarmament norms and in the process exert pressure on the possessor states.

Lifelong Canadian disarmament campaigner Douglas Roche has said that "the anti-nuclear weapons campaign is following the classic lines of other great social movements, such as the end of slavery, colonialism and apartheid: at first, the idea is dismissed by the powerful, then when the idea starts to take hold, it is vigorously objected to until, by persistence, the idea enters the norm of public thinking and laws start to be changed." Countries should ensure they end up on the right side of history by adopting laws that strengthen and speed up the global effort to prohibit and eliminate nuclear weapons.

16

The Tools for Nuclear Disarmament Are Available

Dan Plesch

Dan Plesch is director of the Centre for International Studies and Diplomacy at the School of Oriental and African Studies (SOAS) of the University of London. His research focuses on the UN and disarmament, and he is the author of Human Rights After Hitler.

Though the international community rallied around conflict avoidance and disarmament in the past, in recent years world leaders have undermined these goals. This viewpoint was originally published before the US withdrew from the Intermediate-Range Nuclear Forces Treaty (INF Treaty) and the treaty expired without renewal in February 2019, which has only worsened the situation. However, UN Secretary-General Antonio Guterres has presented a plan on how to reinvigorate disarmament talks among world leaders. It remains to be seen whether UN member states will adopt his recommendations, but the tools are in place to bring about global disarmament.

A network of global institutions were created in 1945 to try and avert another global conflict. They have been gradually undermined over the last 20 years, and now we see them being trashed wholesale. The world leaders responsible are perhaps best described by General Jack D. Ripper in Stanley Kubrick's

"Nuclear Disarmament Is Crucial for Global Security—It Shouldn't Have to Wait," by Dan Plesch, The Conversation, July 12, 2018, https://theconversation.com/nuclear-disarmament-is-crucial-for-global-security-it-shouldnt-have-to-wait-99550.

Dr Strangelove: "They have neither the time nor inclination for strategic thought." The latest round of top-level summits and meetings have duly been coloured by a very real fear of war—but it doesn't have to be this way.

This year's NATO Summit and the upcoming Trump-Putin Summit in Helsinki present the best opportunities in years for today's leaders to emulate their more distinguished predecessors, who understood that disarmament and arms control were prerequisites for the enhancement of national security and international stability.

At the height of the Cold War in the 1980s, NATO Summit declarations were full of debate on arms control and disarmament. And back in 1986, the Reagan-Gorbachev summit in Reykjavik resulted in one of the greatest disarmament achievements of the last century: the Intermediate-Range Nuclear Forces Treaty (INF), which helped dramatically reduce US-Soviet tensions in Europe. But this year's NATO summit began with an openly acrimonious exchange over the allies' relative defence spending, and the US and Russia have both threatened to withdraw from the INF altogether.

Outside of the North Korea-US talks, disarmament and nuclear arms control are all but left out of today's high-level summits. All the while, the global arms control architecture is falling apart, global military expenditure is at its highest since the fall of the Berlin Wall, and the potential nuclear flashpoints in Europe, the Middle East and the South China Sea are multiplying. In a climate like this, what hope is there for eliminating the nuclear threat altogether?

Another Way

The challenge has been taken up by the UN secretary general, Antonio Guterres, who recently issued a document entitled Securing Our Common Future. This is an inspiring, visionary document produced after extensive consultations with governments and civil society. For those with no prior knowledge but now seeking less military solutions to global and regional problems, it's an introduction and a handbook to the hows and whys of disarmament—a rough guide to world peace, if you will.

In clear terms, Guterres surveys the potential for world disarmament, everything from "hand grenades to hydrogen bombs." He argues that the instability and dangers in international affairs should provide an impetus for disarmament—a direct challenge to the five nuclear-armed members of the UN Security Council, who typically argue that peace should be established before disarmament can be seriously entertained.

To tackle this line of thinking, Guterres poses a simple question: do the leaders of the nuclear powers agree with Reagan and Gorbachev that nuclear war by definition cannot be won, and therefore must not be fought?

Guterres' agenda could not be more timely, and never has the UN secretariat produced such a substantive document on disarmament. If the whole of the UN infrastructure integrated disarmament into its work with the support of its member states, that could change the game profoundly. But will the member states heed Guterres's call? Will civil and political society rally to his banner, or simply remain on the sidelines and wring their hands while nothing is done?

A Rusty Toolbox

Some critics point to the Guterres plan's lack of detailed technical action points, and many will hesitate to accept its ambition to be truly comprehensive. But it should be understood as a rallying cry, an attempt to bring together different constituencies which don't usually work together.

Missing this opportunity will further reinforce the status quo—and that in turn might have dire consequences. It's hard to think of a scenario where the militarisation of international relations contributes to stablity and security rather than making the world less safe.

Guterres's agenda is a handbook for those who want to find a way out of the gathering chaos. Disarmament progress in tense geopolitical times is not impossible. In previous times of crisis, rival superpowers have taken steps to reduce arsenals, increase transparency, lower alert levels and mitigate risks. If today's major players wait indefinitely for security conditions to be "ripe" before pursuing disarmament and arms control, the resulting lack of dialogue will only make the climate worse.

Disarmament talks need not start from scratch. Many of the tools are tried and tested, and have simply fallen out of use, with past agreements long overdue for implementation and negotiations on strategic arms stalled. If nations fail to honour their existing commitments, they will not only put the entire disarmament and arms control regime at risk, but also damage the mechanisms designed to defuse tensions and foster dialogue on sensitive security issues.

It's time to return to the common ground on which we stood in the past, the ground where world-changing multilateral and bilateral treaties were struck. Notwithstanding the events leading up to the 2003 invasion of Iraq, the UN-sanctioned inspection regimes provide a sound technical blueprint for verified elimination of weapons of mass destruction. The OSCE's various agreements, confidence- and security-building measures, and "open skies" regime provide an institutional platform for the exchange of information, verification and regulation of conventional weaponry.

While they certainly need updating, the precision tools needed for disarmament and conventional arms control are readily available. What's needed now is the political impetus to use them. The Guterres agenda offers an optimistic way forward at a deeply pessimistic moment; it must be taken seriously.

17

Mass Mobilization Against Nuclear War Worked in the Past and Can Work Now

Duncan Meisel

Duncan Meisel is a Brooklyn-based climate activist and writer.

In this viewpoint, Duncan Meisel interviews the historian Lawrence Wittner about the anti-nuclear movement that took place during the Cold War. He examines the factors that drove mobilization in the past and how they compare to factors today. He argues that these historical campaigns were effective at limiting the damage done by nuclear weapons and asserts that similar strategies could also be effective today. Although past mass mobilizations were largely successful, Meisel and Wittner note that they ultimately failed at the goal of disarmament, and Wittner offers a theory as to why this may be the case.

The Trump administration is reviving the threat of nuclear war in a way that no other US presidency has done since the Cold War.

While the confrontation with North Korea's expanding nuclear and ballistic missile program has taken center stage, Trump's ham-fisted engagement with Taiwan, missile strikes against the Russia-linked Assad regime in Syria and the rapid push for a nuclear

"Mass Mobilization Stopped Nuclear War Before and It Can Again," by Duncan Meisel, Waging Nonviolence, September 5, 2017, https://wagingnonviolence.org/2017/09/mass-mobilization-stopped-nuclear-war/.

weapons modernization program all contribute to a new and unique climate of nuclear threats.

It's easy to feel disempowered in the face of such chaotic and consequential decisions, but the history of nuclear weapons since 1945 is one of extensive and frequent interventions by organized people in the United States and other countries to stop nuclear weapons deployments and nuclear war itself.

No one knows this history better than Lawrence Wittner, professor of history emeritus at SUNY/Albany and author of the three-volume work "The Struggle Against the Bomb." His work explains how—time and again, for over 50 years—one the world's largest social movements used globally organized outrage to pull leaders with little moral compunction back from the brink of using the deadliest weapons on earth.

I recently spoke with Wittner about his seminal research to gain a better understanding of how the nuclear disarmament movement organized its most successful campaigns, how the world might be different without them and the lessons they offer a new generation that seeks to make the world a safer, saner place.

How determined were military leaders to use atomic weapons in various conflicts during the Cold War?

They didn't take nuclear war lightly, but they certainly considered using nuclear weapons many times. Of course, the US government used them rather casually during the Second World War. Japan was on the verge of surrender, and numerous US military leaders told President Truman that he should not use them—including Gen. Eisenhower.

Once Eisenhower came to power, his administration developed the policy of "massive retaliation," which meant that any aggression—nuclear or conventional—by the Soviet bloc in Europe would be met with nuclear war. The NATO policy was to respond to a conventional invasion of Western Europe with a nuclear first strike.

Use of nuclear weapons was considered by the Eisenhower administration during the Korean war and in defense of Chiang Kai-Shek's Nationalist regime on Taiwan and other offshore islands. During the Vietnam War, the Nixon administration talked rather casually about waging nuclear war in Vietnam—or at least Nixon did. He ran this by Kissinger, who was horrified, but Nixon said he was just trying to get him to think creatively.

Then there was the case of the Reagan administration, which came into office talking quite glibly of waging nuclear war and was met by massive opposition.

What stopped government officials from taking nuclear action?

I think their inclinations were challenged and blunted by popular protest against the bomb, which had made nuclear war so abhorrent to the public across the world, including in the United States, that they backed off their plans.

There were several retreats from the hawkish positions government officials had taken, and in some cases a dramatic turnaround. The Eisenhower administration never planned to halt nuclear testing since it assumed that US national security was based on making advances in nuclear weapons. However, in 1958—when it was boxed in by popular protest against nuclear testing—the administration halted US nuclear testing without any treaty, and began negotiations with the British and Soviet governments on a test ban treaty.

During the 1950s, Eisenhower was confronted by Defense Department officials who said they had to get ready to use nuclear weapons to win small wars. They had long feared they couldn't win a war in Asia fought with conventional weapons, and that was true—and therefore the only way they could win it was by employing nuclear weapons. Eisenhower and [Secretary of State] John Foster Dulles both responded, essentially: "We'd like to give you a green light, but the public won't stand for it."

In his book "Danger and Survival," McGeorge Bundy—national security advisor to Kennedy and Johnson and an occasional advisor to Nixon—said that the US government didn't back off waging nuclear war in Vietnam based on the fear of retaliation by the Soviet Union or China, but rather because the world public wouldn't stand for it. Popular opinion against nuclear weapons was so strong, the US government would lose more than it would gain by using them. The public in the US in particular wouldn't stand for it.

The most dramatic example, however, involves the Reagan Administration. Reagan came to the White House as a very hawkish candidate, talking glibly about waging nuclear war. He had opposed every nuclear arms treaty signed by his predecessors. But thanks to the massive nuclear freeze campaign in the United States and the disarmament campaigns overseas, he retreated, and ultimately he adopted nuclear disarmament as a key part of his public policy. He began to say that a "nuclear war can never be won and must never be fought," which was clearly an attempt to head off a popular movement.

What were the things that drove peaks of mobilization against nuclear weapons? How did organizers take advantage of geo-political developments to grow?

The atomic bombings of Hiroshima and Nagasaki were very dramatic, and they were the most significant factors generating initial disgust with nuclear weapons and the desire to abolish them. The fear of nuclear war was great after 1945, and the groups that formed in those first years played on the horror of the bombings and their devastation.

The second dramatic growth took place in late 1950s and early 1960s, largely due to hydrogen bomb tests. They were symbolic of doom in two ways. First, they were a quantum-leap forward in power: They could be made a thousand times as powerful as the bomb that destroyed Hiroshima. The public testing of these weapons symbolized the fate of the world, if they were ever used in war. And who could say they wouldn't be?

Also the H-bomb tests themselves were sending vast clouds of fallout around the world. The scientist Linus Pauling estimated that 1 million people would die from fallout unless tests were halted. For many people nuclear war was rather abstract—it wasn't being waged against them. But these explosions were occurring all the time, and people were being bombarded by radiation that was causing birth defects and cancer. Therefore, it wasn't just war they had to fear, but the tests themselves.

Another mobilization peak took place in the late 1970s through the early 1980s, and that developed out of the revival of the Cold War that seemed to be on the decline after 1963. But Cold War détente was swept away by Reagan in the United States and Thatcher in Britain and Soviet leaders building new nuclear weapons and talking rather glibly about waging nuclear war. Peace groups could play on this theme and assail Reagan in particular as the "Mad Bomber," the man who would unleash nuclear war. In place of nuclear threats and weapons buildups, peace groups demanded a halt to the nuclear arms race as the first step in building a nuclear weapons-free world.

Conversely, what accounts for the valleys of organizing? When did the movement shrink?

The fear of nuclear weapons hadn't gone away by the late 1940s, but there was little hope of getting rid of them thanks to the heightening Cold War. People also feared speaking up in the climate of being labeled subversives.

Another decline came after 1963 when there was growing public complacency thanks to the signing of the Atmospheric Test Ban Treaty. There was also the Vietnam War, which drew people's attention away from the nuclear conflict and towards the US government's assault on this poor, third world nation. The major constituency for the nuclear abolition campaign was the peace movement, and the peace movement had moved to focusing on Vietnam. A lot of people simply turned away from the disarmament campaign and assumed their governments were solving the nuclear problem and could deal with other issues.

A third decline came in the late 1980s, and has continued right up to the present. That was based to some degree on complacency—after all, the US and Soviet governments had resolved their differences, signed treaties, the Cold War came to an end, and the fear of nuclear war went down. But there was also some degree of exhaustion: By the late 1980s people had been campaigning for a decade or more, and so there was a desire to cultivate one's own garden and let world leaders deal with the remaining nuclear dangers.

A common thread running through the entire post-1945 period is that people don't want to think about nuclear war. When they're forced to think of it, when they can't escape it, they want to stop it. But when it's not in the headlines any more and governments are growing more reasonable, they'd just as well not think about it. If nuclear war did break out today, you can bet more people would focus on it, but, of course, we don't want that war to have to take place.

The peace movement's challenge is to maintain its momentum and sense of danger—even though the world might seem safer and there are fewer nuclear weapons in the world. If the nations of the world are maintaining their arsenals, the struggle hasn't come to an end.

Do you think the moment we're experiencing today with Trump and North Korea is potentially a driving force for another peak of movement energy? What's different today?

It's possible that there will be some revival of the nuclear disarmament movement, but we haven't seen the surge of resistance yet. I'm a co-chair of the national board of the group Peace Action, so I'm very well aware of how peace groups are doing. While Peace

Action isn't doing badly, we're certainly not yet experiencing the surge of action in the streets, such as when its predecessors, SANE and the Nuclear Freeze Campaign, were taking off.

One reason it's not taking place is that the mass media rarely focus on the danger of nuclear war, and when they do focus on it, it's the danger of some other country waging war on the United States. One day it's Iran, another day it's North Korea—but they don't seem to get to the basic problem that nine countries have 15,000 nuclear weapons in their arsenals. It's a worldwide phenomenon, as is the persistence of the idea of nuclear weapons as the ultimate guarantor of national security.

Right now there's also a sense that only Koreans are vulnerable, that most Americans aren't at risk of being bombarded by nuclear missiles. At the height of popular protest in the 1980s, millions of people were in the streets—in part because US and Soviet arsenals could reach both sides quite easily. That got people to wake up and realize that nuclear war wasn't such a hot idea after all.

How big a role did fear play in these spikes of organizing? How can people dealing with fear of the Trump administration, or of North Korean nuclear mobilization, help direct that energy into making nuclear conflict less likely?

I think fear has probably been the most important factor in mobilizing people. When you look at things psychologically, people should be afraid of nuclear weapons and nuclear war. It seems irrational to go bury your head in the sand and not worry about them.

But it's also true, in two ways, that fear is dangerous. One is that it can be demobilizing, that people get so scared they're scared silent. They become so frightened they retreat and they don't feel powerful any more. They might take drugs instead of taking action.

A second danger is that, if people are scared of nuclear war, the hawks have an answer for them. They turn fear on its head: Yes, they say, nuclear war could be a bad thing, that's why we need nuclear weapons to deter the bad Russians, Iranians, North Koreans and so on. This means fear may reinforce the desire for nuclear weapons rather than for getting rid of them.

For these reasons, the use of nuclear fear has to be very careful. Peace activists have to make the case that as long as nuclear weapons exist there's no real security from nuclear war, and therefore we need to get rid of nuclear weapons. That's the best case that can be made by nuclear disarmament forces: The arms race is a race no one wins.

What are some of the forgotten "paths not taken" of weapons not built or decisions not made as a result of anti-nuclear organizing? How might the world be different if those things had been built?

The neutron bomb was being proposed during the Carter administration. This enhanced radiation weapon was designed to destroy people rather than property, and was scheduled by the Carter administration to be deployed in Western European nations. But once peace groups learned of it and began to focus on its terrible effects, this caused massive protests in Western European nations and, eventually, an unwillingness to support the neutron bomb deployment by their government officials. As a result, the Carter administration finally concluded that, if Western governments weren't willing to stand up for it, the US government wasn't going to be the villain of the piece. So Carter canceled plans for its deployment.

The MX missile was the jewel in the crown of the Reagan administration during its first term of office. Peace groups said that it was a first-strike weapon, and there was so much popular protest against it that Reagan couldn't get funding through Congress. Eventually, a plan that began as 200 missiles barely slipped through with 50 missiles. That failure became the basis of the US government's push for strategic arms reduction treaties, for it meant the US government couldn't keep pace with development of intercontinental ballistic missiles. And the next best thing was seeing to it that neither country had those weapons. The best way to do that was to sign a treaty: the Strategic Arms Reduction Treaty, or START, which Gorbachev welcomed and showed him, in many ways, to be a peace person, strongly influenced by the movement.

Gorbachev had his own peace-oriented ideas, but he also received a large amount of information from the disarmament movement in the United States and around the world. He would take time out of his meetings with heads of state to meet with representatives of groups like the Freeze campaign, SANE, and International Physicians for the Prevention of Nuclear War. So, Gorbachev and Reagan's detente and the overall drawback from the nuclear brink were heavily influenced by the peace movement — not just through public pressure but also through direct engagement.

Are there other potentially winnable campaigns of this kind available to anti-nuclear weapons activists today that might limit the likelihood of the Trump administration using nuclear weapons?

It seems to me there are two ways to develop mass pressure on Trump and Congress in connection with the general problem of nuclear weapons.

The first has to do with the trillion dollar nuclear "modernization" program — the plan to upgrade the entire nuclear weapons complex, build new bombers and missiles and submarines and so on. That cost is so great that it provides the opportunity to reach people who are already concerned about the arms race or are satisfied with the weapons we already have and don't want to bankrupt the country. So you can make demands for cutbacks in the "modernization" plan or stopping it entirely and mobilize a sympathetic constituency.

A second way is to focus on Trump's mental instability: The fact that he's a reckless, dangerous leader, who really shouldn't have the button to launch nuclear war in his hand. That's what the currently proposed Markey-Lieu bill seeks to address: Under its provisions, unless there's a nuclear attack on the United States, the president cannot initiate nuclear war without a Congressional declaration of war. Since Congress hasn't declared war since 1941, that's a pretty big restriction.

Sen. Markey also introduced the SANE act, which provides for a massive cutback in the trillion dollar nuclear weapons program. These are two bills that Peace Action is supporting right now.

What role did collaboration with people on the frontlines of nuclear weapons production, testing and usage play in the successes of the movement?

Hibakusha, the victims who survived the Hiroshima and Nagasaki bombings, have played a very significant role—their testimony and example inspired people around the world.

Certainly, atmospheric nuclear tests, which were sending vast clouds of fallout around the world, had a major impact in terms of people nearest the sites. People in those communities in Nevada and Utah grew very wary and filed lawsuits against the federal government for damages.

Groups of veterans got together and formed atomic veterans associations, for many members of the armed forces had been sent to testing sites to get them ready for nuclear war. They were given very little protection. When they began to die from cancer or had children with birth defects, they filed lawsuits. This became another major headache for the US government, and helped expand the constituency of the nuclear disarmament movement.

Then there were people working at or near uranium mining sites. Massive cancer outbreaks occurred among miners, who were often Native Americans. Their sacred land was being polluted and destroyed, and they began dying of cancer. They told horrifying stories and linked up with the nuclear free community movement.

Nuclear weapons production sites contaminated vast regions: the Hanford Nuclear Weapons Site is a nightmare. Finding something to do with nuclear waste is still a major problem. People living near these sites provided a massive cancer cluster, suffered terribly from the nuclear production process, and became active in the anti-nuclear campaign. By the 1980s and 1990s there were campaigns in these communities working in cooperation with peace groups that shut down many of these production sites.

The most stunning success, in my opinion, of the anti-nuclear weapons movement is the push for a Nuclear Freeze and the effect it had on ending the Cold War. What happened through the '80s with the Nuclear Freeze movement and how did that contribute to the end of this incredibly deadly standoff?

I should start by saying that while there was certainly a very powerful Freeze movement in the United States, the movement in the rest of the world was not based on a nuclear freeze—it was based on abolishing nuclear weapons. There was some tension between the Freeze campaign in the United States and the other movements, such as Campaign for Nuclear Disarmament in Britain, which called for banning the bomb.

The Freeze was a bilateral halt to the testing, development and deployment of nuclear weapons by the Soviet Union and United States. It was proposed by Randall Forsberg, who was a defense and disarmament expert. She wanted some kind of focus for the movement, which was engaged in diverse projects at the time. So she proposed the Freeze idea to a variety of peace groups and, though some of the more militant peace groups were wary, the major ones went for it and meetings spread to localities across the United States.

Different groups contributed their resources to it, but there was also an independent Nuclear Weapons Freeze Campaign that developed. It began to introduce and win propositions in favor of the Freeze in local town councils and state legislatures because people thought it made perfect sense. Polls showed that 72 percent of the American public backed it. Occasionally, these ballot propositions and city resolutions failed, but they mostly passed. Dozens of states, hundreds of towns, associations and groups that hadn't otherwise taken a stand on foreign policy in the past endorsed the Freeze. Members of Congress introduced resolutions into the House and Senate—which the movement actually thought was premature—and the Freeze passed by a substantial majority in the House but not in the Senate, where it was blocked by Republicans.

In subsequent years, the Reagan administration was driven back from its hawkish stance and entered disarmament negotiations with the Soviet Union. While there was no formal Freeze, there were governments that refused to accept cruise and Pershing II missiles. There were governments demanding the United States and Soviet Union get together to disarm. The Reagan administration felt itself besieged and began moving towards signing arms control and disarmament agreements.

Testing and deployment was stopped and—under the Intermediate Nuclear Forces Treaty signed in 1987—cruise and Pershing II missiles, as well as Soviet SS20 missiles, were banned from Europe. This was followed by the START treaty, which reduced ICBM numbers on both sides. Before long, Gorbachev and Reagan were strolling around Red Square talking about what good friends they were, and it was by and large the movement that was responsible for that.

What do you think kept the anti-nuclear movement from achieving its final goal of disarmament? What is the lesson for us today?

First, we should recognize that there's been great success in reducing weapons arsenals from their high point of around 70,000 weapons to less than 15,000 today. That's still 15,000 too many—but, nonetheless, looked at over time, that's a real gain.

The central problem, though, is that for thousands of years there's been a reliance on violence and war to solve disputes between competing groups. The assumption among government leaders is that the bigger the weapon, the more security you have—and the public often agrees. How do we counter that? The answer is to develop nonviolent organizations and global institutions that can provide other kinds of security for people.

Nonviolent resistance has been developed over time and popularized by Gandhi and the US civil rights movement. That's one way for people to engage in social struggle without killing other people or otherwise harming them.

On the international level it's vital to have institutions that get nations to back off from conflicts with one another and resolve them short of an arms race and war. It means developing a stronger United Nations that can work to, and hopefully resolve, international disputes.

As long as people feel insecure, they're going to be reluctant to give up their weapons and the option of violence. So we need to develop alternative means of security.

What do you think is next for people working against nuclear weapons? What are your hopes for the future?

I'm a historian. I'm much better at talking about the past than predicting the future. So, I'll focus on what I'd like to see happen. In my opinion, critics of nuclear weapons should convince other people that nuclear weapons provide more problems than they solve, that they are counter-productive. They should convince people that there are better ways to foster security than building nuclear weapons, threatening to use them, and employing them in war. If enough people devote themselves to the nuclear disarmament campaign, we can create a nuclear weapons-free world and prevent nuclear war. We've come part of the way, and we should finish the job.

Organizations to Contact

The editors have compiled the following list of organizations concerned with the issues debated in this book. The descriptions are derived from materials provided by the organizations. All have publications or information available for interested readers. The list was compiled on the date of publication of the present volume; the information provided here may change. Be aware that many organizations take several weeks or longer to respond to inquiries, so allow as much time as possible.

Arms Control Association (ACA)
1200 18th Street NW, Suite 1175
Washington, DC 20036
phone: (202) 463-8270
website: www.armscontrol.org

The ACA is a national nonpartisan membership organization dedicated to promoting public understanding of and support for effective arms control policies.

Belfer Center for Science and International Affairs
79 John F. Kennedy Street
Cambridge, MA 02138
phone: (617) 495-9858
email: sharon_wilke@hks.harvard.edu
website: www.belfercenter.org

The Belfer Center is the hub of Harvard Kennedy School's research, teaching, and training in international security and diplomacy, environmental and resource issues, and science and technology policy.

Brazilian-Argentine Agency for Accounting and Control of Nuclear Materials (ABACC)
Av. Rio Branco
123 - Centro
G 515
Rio de Janeiro-RJ 20040-005
Brazil
phone: +55 21 3171 1200
email: info@abacc.org.br
website: www.abacc.org.br/en/

The principal mission of the ABACC is to guarantee for Argentina, Brazil, and the international community that all existing nuclear materials and facilities in the two countries are being used exclusively for peaceful purposes.

British American Security Information Council (BASIC)
The Foundry
17 Oval Way
Vauxhall
London SE11 5RR
United Kingdom
phone: +44(0) 020 3752 5662
email: basicuk@basicint.org
website: www.basicint.org

BASIC promotes dialogue to advance national security and believes that international peace can be achieved through cooperation rather than threat.

Campaign for Nuclear Disarmament (CND)
162 Holloway Road
London N7 8DQ
United Kingdom
phone: +44 020 7700 2393
email: enquiries@cnduk.org
website: www.cnduk.org

The CND leads nonviolent campaigns to rid the world of nuclear weapons and other weapons of mass destruction to create genuine security for future generations. CND opposes all nuclear and other weapons of mass destruction, including their development, manufacture, testing, deployment, and use or threatened use by any country.

Department of Energy (DOE)
1000 Independence Avenue SW
Washington, DC 20585
phone: (202) 586-4403
email: The.Secretary@hq.doe.gov
website: www.energy.gov

The mission of the Department of Energy is to ensure America's security and prosperity by addressing its energy, environmental, and nuclear challenges through transformative science and technology solutions.

European Nuclear Society (ENS)
Avenue des Arts 56
1000 Brussels
Belgium
phone: +32 2 505 30 50
email: info@euronuclear.org
website: euronuclear.org

ENS promotes the development of nuclear science and technology and the understanding of peaceful nuclear applications. Founded in 1975, ENS is the largest society for nuclear science, research, and industry in Europe.

Federation of American Scientists (FAS)
1112 16th Street NW
Suite 400
Washington, DC 20036
phone: (202) 546-3300
email: fas@fas.org
website: www.fas.org

FAS provides scientific analysis and solutions to protect against catastrophic threats to national and international security. It works to reduce the spread of nuclear weapons, prevent nuclear terrorism, and elevate standards for nuclear energy safety.

Institute of Nuclear Materials Management (INMM)
1120 Rte. 73
Suite 200
Mount Laurel, NJ 08054
phone: (856) 380-6813
website: www.inmm.org

The INMM is dedicated to the safe, secure, and effective stewardship of nuclear materials and related technologies through the advancement of scientific knowledge, technical skills, policy dialogue, professional capabilities, and best practices.

International Atomic Energy Agency (IAEA)
Vienna International Centre
PO Box 100
A-1400 Vienna
Austria
phone: +43 1 2600-0
website: www.iaea.org

IAEA is the world's central intergovernmental forum for scientific and technical cooperation in the nuclear field. It works for the safe, secure, and peaceful use of nuclear science and technology.

Nuclear Threat Initiative (NTI)
1776 Eye Street NW
Suite 600
Washington, DC 20006
phone: (202) 296-4810
email: contact@nyi.org
website: www.nti.org

The NTI is a nonpartisan, nonprofit organization founded in 2001 that works to prevent catastrophic attacks and accidents with weapons of mass destruction and disruption—including nuclear, biological, radiological, chemical, and cyber weapons.

Stimson Center
1211 Connecticut Avenue NW
8th Floor
Washington, DC 20036
phone: (202) 478-3437
email: communications@stimson.org
website: www.stimson.org

The Stimson Center is a nonpartisan policy research center working to protect people, preserve the planet, and promote security and prosperity. Stimson's award-winning research serves as a roadmap to address borderless threats through concerted action.

World Association of Nuclear Operators (WANO)
Level 35
25 Canada Square
Canary Wharf
London, E14 5LQ
United Kingdom
phone: +44 (0)20 7478 9200
website: www.wano.info

WANO exists purely to help nuclear operators accomplish the highest levels of operational safety and reliability. This is achieved through a series of peer reviews, access to technical support, and a global library of operating experience.

World Institute for Nuclear Security (WINS)
Landstrasser
Hauptstrasse 1
1030 Vienna
Austria
phone: +43 1 710 6519
email: info@wins.org
website: www.wins.org

WINS is a nongovernmental membership organization that is committed to building an international community of professionals who are demonstrably competent and willing to work together to strengthen the security of nuclear materials.

World Nuclear Association (WNA)
Tower House
10 Southampton Street
London, WC2E 7HA
United Kingdom
phone: +44 (0)20 7451 1520
email: info@world-nuclear.org
website: www.world-nuclear.org

The WNA is an international organization that represents the global nuclear industry. Its mission is to promote a wider understanding of nuclear energy among key international influencers by providing authoritative information, developing common industry positions, and contributing to the energy debate.

Bibliography

Books

Avner Cohen. *Israel and the Bomb*. New York, NY: Columbia University Press, 1999.

Andrew Futter. *Hacking the Bomb: Cyber Threats and Nuclear Weapons*. New York, NY: Simon and Schuster, 2017.

Garrett Graff. *Raven Rock: The Story of the US Government's Secret Plan to Save Itself—While the Rest of Us Die*. New York, NY: Simon and Schuster, 2017.

John Hershey. *Hiroshima*. New York, NY: A. A. Knopf, 1946.

Herman Kahn. *On Thermonuclear War*. New York, NY: Free Press, 1969.

Jeffrey Lewis. *The Minimum Means of Reprisal: China's Search for Security in the Nuclear Age*. Cambridge, MA: The MIT Press, 2007.

George Perkovich. *India's Nuclear Bomb: The Impact on Global Proliferation*. Berkeley, CA: University of California Press, 2001.

Brad Roberts. *The Case for US Nuclear Weapons in the 21st Century*. Palo Alto, CA: Stanford University Press, 2016.

Scott D. Sagan. *The Limits of Safety: Organizations, Accidents, and Nuclear Weapons*. Princeton, NJ: Princeton University Press, 1995.

Scott D. Sagan and Kenneth N. Waltz. *The Spread of Nuclear Weapons: An Enduring Debate*. New York, NY: W. W. Norton & Co., 2013.

Paul Scharre. *Army of None: Autonomous Weapons and the Future of War*. New York, NY: W. W. Norton & Co., 2018.

Eric Schlosser. *Command and Control: Nuclear Weapons, the Damascus Accident, and the Illusion of Safety*. London, UK: Penguin Books, 2014.

Stephen I. Schwartz. *Atomic Audit: The Costs and Consequences of US Nuclear Weapons Since 1940*. Washington, DC: Brookings Institution Press, 1998.

Adam Stulberg and Matthew Fuhrman. *The Nuclear Renaissance and International Security*. Palo Alto, CA: Stanford University Press, 2013.

Spencer Weart. *Nuclear Fear: A History of Images*. Cambridge, MA: Harvard University Press, 1989.

Tom Zoellner. *Uranium: War, Energy and the Rock that Shaped the World*. London, UK: Penguin Books, 2010.

Periodicals and Internet Sources

James E. Cartwright and Vladimir Dvorkin, "How to Avert a Nuclear War," *New York Times*, April 19, 2015, https://www.nytimes.com/2015/04/20/opinion/how-to-avert-a-nuclear-war.html?searchResultPosition=8.

Doug Bock Clark, "How Civilian Firms Fact-Check North Korea's Denuclearization Efforts," *New Yorker*, February 26, 2019, https://www.newyorker.com/news/news-desk/how-civilian-firms-fact-check-north-koreas-denuclearization-efforts.

Adam Entous, "How Trump and Three Other US Presidents Protected Israel's Worst-Kept Secret: Its Nuclear Arsenal," *New Yorker*, June 18, 2018, https://www.newyorker.com/news/news-desk/how-trump-and-three-other-us-presidents-protected-israels-worst-kept-secret-its-nuclear-arsenal.

Brian Gallagher, "Why a Post-Nuclear World Would Look Nothing Like 'Mad Max,'" *Nautilus*, June 27, 2015, http://

nautil.us/blog/-why-a-post_nuclear-world-would-look-nothing-like-mad-max.

Mikhail Gorbachev, "The Madness of Nuclear Deterrence," *Wall Street Journal*, April 29, 2019, https://www.wsj.com/articles/the-madness-of-nuclear-deterrence-11556577762?mod=searchresults&page=1&pos=2.

Sam Haselby, "The Deterrence Myth," *Aeon*, January 9, 2018, https://aeon.co/essays/nuclear-deterrence-is-more-ideology-than-theory.

Martin Kaste, "Who Should Warn the Public of Nuclear War?" NPR, February 12, 2018, https://www.npr.org/2018/02/12/584688294/who-should-warn-the-public-of-nuclear-war.

Robert Klara, "Nuclear Fallout Shelters Were Never Going to Work," *History*, September 1, 2018, https://www.history.com/news/nuclear-fallout-shelters-were-never-going-to-work.

John Krzyzaniak, "No, Iran Didn't Exit the Nuclear Deal. And No, Its Nuclear Announcement Is not Revenge for Soleimani," *Bulletin of the Atomic Scientists,* January 6, 2020, https://thebulletin.org/2020/01/no-iran-didnt-exit-the-nuclear-deal-and-no-its-nuclear-announcement-is-not-revenge-for-soleimani/.

Sylvie Lanteaume and Kerry Sheridan, "Fake News Among Threats Keeping Doomsday Clock at Two Minutes to Midnight," *Times of Israel,* January 24, 2019, https://www.timesofisrael.com/fake-news-among-threats-keeping-doomsday-clock-at-two-minutes-to-midnight/.

John Mecklin, "Why Nuclear Weapons Should Be a Major Focus of the 2020 Campaign," *Bulletin of the Atomic Scientists,* January 13, 2020, https://www.tandfonline.com/doi/full/10.1080/00963402.2019.1702274.

Susan Moeller, "Weapons of Mass Destruction and the Media: Anatomy of a Failure," YaleGlobal Online, April 14, 2004, https://yaleglobal.yale.edu/content/weapons-mass-destruction-and-media-anatomy-failure.

Adam Mount and Richard Nephew, "A Nuclear Weapons Ban Should First Do No Harm to the NPT," *Bulletin of the Atomic Scientists*, March 7, 2017, https://thebulletin.org/2017/03/a-nuclear-weapons-ban-should-first-do-no-harm-to-the-npt/.

Ron Rosenbaum, "Trump's Nuclear Experience," *Slate*, March 1, 2016, http://www.slate.com/articles/news_and_politics/the_spectator/2016/03/trump_s_nuclear_experience_advice_for_reagan_in_1987.html.

George P. Shultz, William J. Perry, and Sam Nunn, "The Threat of Nuclear War Is Still with Us," *Wall Street Journal,* April 10, 2019, https://www.wsj.com/articles/the-threat-of-nuclear-war-is-still-with-us-11554936842?mod=searchresults&page=1&pos=1.

David Welna, "The End May Be Nearer: Doomsday Clock Moves Within 100 Seconds of Midnight," NPR, January 23, 2020, https://www.npr.org/2020/01/23/799047659/the-end-may-be-nearer-doomsday-clock-moves-within-100-seconds-of-midnight.

Joshua Williams, "The Quick and the Dead," Carnegie Endowment for International Peace, June 16, 2005, https://carnegieendowment.org/publications/index.cfm?fa=view&id=17078&prog=zgp&proj=znpp.

Aron Woonink, "Is Japan's 'Nuclear Allergy' Being Cured?" the *Diplomat*, December 2, 2017, https://thediplomat.com/2017/12/is-japans-nuclear-allergy-being-cured/.

Index

K

M

N

O

P

R

S

T

U

V

W

9